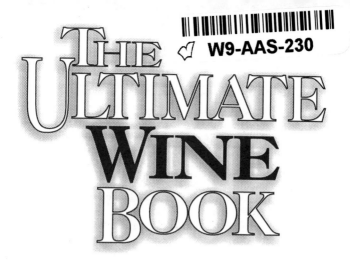

THE ULTIMATE WINE BOOK

*Everything you need
to know about
wine appreciation,
wine with food, and the
latest health findings*

By Don W. Martin and
Betty Woo Martin, PharmD

Foreword by Robert Mondavi

Pine Cone Press ● Henderson, Nevada

2

BOOKS BY DON AND BETTY MARTIN

Adventure Cruising ● 1996
Arizona Discovery Guide ● 1990, 1994, 1996
Arizona in Your Future ● 1991, 1993, 1998
Best of the Gold Country ● 1987, 1990, 1992
Best of San Francisco ● 1986, 1990, 1994, 1997
Best of the Wine Country ● 1991, 1994, 1995, 2000
California–Nevada Roads Less Traveled ● 1999
Inside San Francisco ● 1991
Las Vegas: The Best of Glitter City ● 1998, 2000
Nevada Discovery Guide ● 1992, 1997
New Mexico Discovery Guide ● 1998
Northern California Discovery Guide ● 1993
Oregon Discovery Guide ● 1993, 1995, 1996, 1999
San Diego: The Best of Sunshine City ● 1999
San Francisco's Ultimate Dining Guide ● 1988
The Toll-free Traveler ● 1997
The Ultimate Wine Book ● 1993, 1999
Utah Discovery Guide ● 1995
Washington Discovery Guide ● 1994, 1997, 2000

Copyright © 2000 by Don W. Martin and Betty Woo Martin

All rights reserved. No part of this book may be reproduced in any form, other than brief passages in book reviews, without written permission from the authors. Manufactured in the United States of America.

Library of Congress Cataloging-in-Publication Data:

Martin, Don and Betty—
The Ultimate Wine Book
Includes index.

1. Wine—tasting and appreciation; uses with food; wine and health

ISBN: 0-942053-29-X

Library of Congress catalog card number 93-84914

Cover design & inside artwork ● **Bob Shockley**

This book is dedicated, with deep gratitude, to the authors of the Twenty-first Amendment to the Constitution of the United States of America.

FOREWORD

I first met Don Martin in 1971 when he was researching an article about our winery, which was then one of the newest in the Napa Valley. We were starting the Mondavi Summer Festivals and I recall discussing with him our belief that wine and cultural activities complement each other, as part of the good life.

This book follows their common-sense outlook, that people should spend more time enjoying life and the good things it brings, such as wine, and less time worrying about it.

Here in the Napa Valley, it's easy to understand the pleasures of wine. Unfortunately, some people in the "wine world" have made it ridiculously complicated to enjoy one of life's most intriguing pleasures. To really appreciate wine, all you need to know is what the various wines taste like and what foods go with them. With the help of simple, practical books like Don and Betty's, and a lot of tasting, almost everyone will find a wine they like!

We view wine as an integral part of our culture, heritage and gracious way of life. For us, wine is the temperate, civilized, sacred, romantic beverage recommended in the Bible. Wine has been praised for centuries by physicians, statesmen, philosophers, poets and scholars. It has been with us since civilization began. It will be with us indefinitely, despite efforts by neo-prohibitionists to convince us that wine is not a good thing.

Fortunately, the medical community has made many discoveries confirming the health benefits of moderate wine consumption. The Martins have devoted considerable study to this. Please read this book's section on wine and health carefully. We think you will be pleased to discover that something as good as wine also is good for you!

The world of wine is a continually fascinating, educational and enjoyable one, and we vintners encourage you to sample it. Read books about wine, visit our wineries, and most of all, taste.

To your health.
Robert Mondavi

> *WARNING:* When taken as directed, wine enhances food, reduces stress, encourages camaraderie, enlivens conversation and kindles romance. Used in moderation, it has been shown to aid digestion, protect the heart, promote good health and improve one's disposition. Recommended dosage is one to two glasses per day, preferably with meals. Excessive usage is unwise, potentially unhealthy and decidedly uncilivized.

CONTENTS

PART I: THIS CIVILIZED BEVERAGE
1. *Wine: What it is and where it came from — 12*
2. *Kinds of wines: What's behind those labels — 29*
3. *Finding vines: Visiting America's winelands — 58*
4. *Appreciating wines: What if I don't like it? — 92*

PART II: THIS HEALTHY BEVERAGE
5. *Wine and health: A very old idea whose time has come — 112*
6. *Les Paradoxe Français: Goose liver paté and longevity, too? — 118*
7. *A California Curve? What the American surveys tell us — 121*
SPECIAL: *Ten keys to healthy living — 130*
8. *A medical View: Hearts and other parts — 131*
9. *The right measure: Wine use without abuse — 149*

PART III: WINE AND YOUR DIET
10. *Matching food and wine; wine as a food; wine and cooking — 156*
11. La Mediteranee: *The diet for life — 164*
12. *Afterthoughts: A glossary of wine terms; additional reading — 176*

ASSORTED GRAPHICS
Sample wine label — 34
California wine regions map — 61
Oregon wine regions map — 81
Washington wine regions map — 85
New York wine regions map — 89
Winetasting scorecard — 100
Mortality rate ("J-Curve") chart — 123
World longevity chart — 128
Mediterranean diet pyramid — 166

INTRODUCTION
to the revised edition

This book and a bottle of good Zinfandel are all you need to understand and appreciate fine wine.

My wife and I began the original *Ultimate Wine Book*, several years ago with two good reference books, a bottle of Pedroncelli Zin and a plate of Nabisco Wheat Thins between us. My book of choice was Justin Meyer's *Plain Talk About Fine Wine*; hers was Dr. Salvatore P. Lucia's *Wine and Your Well-Being*.

Our intention was to research and write a book that would immodestly live up to its presumptuous title. Libraries have been written in defense of wine, in definition of wine, in praise of wine and—in recent years—in support of wine as a healthful beverage. Why not, we thought, tuck all of this information, adoration and speculation into a single, thin and relatively inexpensive volume? Something that would fit into purse, glove compartment or Levi hip pocket.

We decided to approach this subject on three broad fronts:

I. The history and appreciation of wine.

II. The healthful benefits of this terribly civilized beverage.

III. The happy marriage of wine with food.

The original book met with considerable success. What you now hold in your hands is an updated and revised edition, incorporating the latest information about the world's most honored beverage.

We feel that this book will answer your most-asked questions, that will encourage you to match the reproachful glare of a sommelier with your own steady stare, that will put you at ease in the world of wine.

Leonard S. Bernstein, author of a delightful book called *The Official Guide to Wine Snobbery*, defines the difference between a wine sophisticate and a wine snob: "A wine sophisticate knows that 1970 was a great year for Château Latour. A wine snob knows the name of the cellarmaster."

We are neither. I prefer the term "wine enthusiast." This suggests that I enjoy wine (particularly a good Zinfandel), that I find it to be a fascinating object of study, and that I neither worship nor adore it. My wife, whose Chinese heritage dictates that her interest is more academic than emotional, is none of the above. While she has studied wine and her medical background has contributed significantly to these pages, she is not a wine drinker. These differing attitudes provide the proper balance for our sensible approach to the subject.

There is significance to the tools with which we began this project. Pedroncelli is one of many California vintners producing good, honest, non-presumptuous wines. *Plain Talk About Fine Wine* is one of the most sensible books ever written on the subject, while *Wine and Your Well-Being* was one of the first books to discuss wine's health benefits, written back in 1971.

It will become obvious as you read the chapters ahead that we are defenders of wine; that we oppose any neo-prohibitionist movement to brand it as some sort of dangerous drug. We are troubled by the protectionist government mentality that treats adults as children, insisting that warning labels be placed on virtually everything. (We saw the ultimate warning label on a bottle of sleeping pills recently. It read: "Caution, this product will make you drowsy.")

In late 1991, an episode of CBS's *60 Minutes* pointed out that, although the French drink nine times more wine than Americans, they outlive us. The phenomena became known as the "French Paradox" and it sparked dozens of studies on wine and health.

After a decade of these studies, the medical jury has returned its verdict. Used in moderation, wine is good for us. Not just harmless, but *good* for us. Learn to relax, you government officials, and enjoy the happy news.

Something else will become apparent as you read on. We regard wine and its mystique with a sense of humor. Too often, wine sophisticates, like bureaucrats, take themselves too seriously. This attitude often intimidates people new to wine lore. Our message is as clear as a good Chardonnay: Relax, get a couple of clean glasses, pull a cork and enjoy yourselves.

Don W. Martin
Sipping Zin, somewhere in the wine country

THANK YOU...

Most books are written by committee. Dozens of sources provide the material, while we merely organize it and throw in a few adjectives. This is certainly true of a book of this complexity, since it approaches the fascinating field of wine from several directions.

The original edition of the book and this current revision could not have been written without the assistance of many people. While we alone are responsible for its editorial content and opinions, these folks provided valuable insight and guidance.

We particularly want to thank **Arthur L. Klatsky,** M.D., chief of the Division of Cardiology at the Kaiser Permanente Medical Center in Oakland, California; and **Andrew L. Waterhouse**, Ph.D., assistant professor, Department of Viticulture and Enology, University of California at Davis.

Dr. Klatsky's ongoing studies regarding wine, health and lifestyles are among the most comprehensive and revealing ever conducted and we drew from his studies extensively for our research. He found time in his busy schedule to review key parts of this book, for which we are extremely grateful.

A leading authority on wine's healthful constituents, Dr. Waterhouse provided much useful information for the wine and health portion of this book, then he took the time to review that segment of the manuscript for both the original and revised editions.

Another very important source of information was the **Wine Institute** of San Francisco, the major trade organization of California's wine industry. Through the decades, it has played a significant role in promoting and supporting wine as a healthy, pleasant beverage and an important part of our social fabric. Its director of research and education, **Elisabeth Holmgren,** has been very helpful in providing us with reams of remarkably useful information on the fruit of the grape.

Several other organizations, public and private, also have contributed data to this book, particularly regarding the wine and health issue. Some of these sources are unbiased, concerned primarily with gathering and disseminating information about public health. Others are obviously partial to wine, since they are industry connected or supported. What is significant is that they all have come to the same conclusion: For most people, moderate drinking is a healthy enhancement of life.

We list these organizations with their addresses, in case you want to consult them for additional information: **University of California**, Department of Viticulture and Enology, Davis, CA 95616-8749; **The Wine Institute**, 425 Market St., Suite 1000, San Francisco, CA 94105; **American Council on Science and Health,** 1995 Broadway, Second Floor, New York, NY 10023-5860; **American Wine Alliance for Research and Education,** 244 California St., San Francisco, CA 94111; **Oldways Preservation & Exchange Trust,** 25 First St., Cambridge, MA 02141; **Robert Mondavi Mission Program,** P.O. Box 106, Oakville, CA 94562; and the **National Wine Coalition,** 1575 Eye Street NW, Suite 325, Washington, DC 20005.

A BIT ABOUT THE AUTHORS

Don and Betty Martin have written more than twenty books about wine and travel. When not seeking the ultimate Zinfandel, Don devotes his waking hours to writing, photography and the operation of Pine Cone Press, Inc. Betty does much of the photography, research and editing for their books, and she also has contributed photos and articles to various publications.

The two are eminently qualified to discuss the subject of the grape. Don has studied and written about wine for four decades, and he has "sipped wine with serious intent since the age of consent." Betty has a doctorate in pharmacy and a particular interest in food pharmacology. An expert cook, she has studied wine and food in the Hospitality Management program at California's Columbia College, and she has taken other courses in wine and sensory evaluation.

IS ANYBODY OUT THERE?

This book contains thousands of facts, carefully researched, as well as a few conclusions and an occasional supposition. If you feel we've erred in gathering information, or if you'd like to offer your knowledge for future editions of *The Ultimate Wine Book,* we'd like to hear from you.

This is **not** a medical journal, and should not be regarded as such. It's an appraisal of the pleasures of wine, its health benefits as established by medical authorities, and its use with food. For specifics on the possible effects of your personal use wine or any other alcoholic beverage, consult your physician.

All who contribute useful information for later editions of this text will receive a free copy of one of our other publications, listed in the back of this book.

Address your cards and letters to:

Pine Cone Press
631 N. Stephanie St., PMB 138
Henderson, NV 89014

Quickly bring me a beaker of wine, so that I may whet my mind and say something clever.

— ARISTOPHANES (450-385 B.C.)

Part I:
THIS CIVILIZED BEVERAGE

Prohibitionists say that drinking is bad for you, but the Bible says that Noah made wine and drank it, and he lived to be 950 years old. Show me an abstainer who ever lived that long.
— WILL ROGERS

Chapter one

WINE

What it is
and where it
came from

This book is intended to help you understand, appreciate and enjoy mankind's most civilized beverage. Wine is one of the rarest of things: Not only does it make us feel good, it is good *for* us!

Although we discuss wine and health in this book, it is not our main focus. Primarily, we regard wine as an inviting beverage, long associated with camaraderie and good food, a thing to be enjoyed and shared.

Our intent is not to encourage you to drink wine. If you're an abstainer, or if you prefer a martini to a Merlot, you must have good reasons. However, if you do enjoy wine, this book will help you broaden that enjoyment. It will brush away the mystique and put wine where it belongs—in your glass and not on a pedestal. Also, it will attempt to brush away the guilt that some folks associate with alcohol.

There is an attitude afoot which suggests that if something gives us sensual pleasure, it must be bad for us. It implies that life is little more than a brief tug-of-war between good and evil. And then we die. If we are good, if we work hard and resist temptation, avoid the guilt of pleasure, and obey all those warning labels, we will find our reward in Heaven. If we are naughty, if we pursue pleasure and avoid the discipline of pain, we get a one-way ticket on the down escalator.

America's founding fathers and mothers seemed more preoccupied with the denial of pleasure than the pursuit of it. Indeed, they called themselves Puritans.

Some of their descendants today walk the halls of our legislatures, seeking ways to deliver us from Temptation, or at least put a warning label on it and tax it. To be sure, many of their concerns are valid. Armed with evidence from health professionals, they point out that tobacco in all forms and in any amount is harmful. Asbestos is bad for the lungs, cholesterol is bad for the arteries, and mice should avoid saccharin.

However, when it comes to wine, the signals become confused; the line between Good and Evil is blurred. Puritans say it's bad, yet Jesus likened it to his own blood. Dr. Louis Pasteur, the founder of modern medicine, called it the most healthful and hygienic of all beverages.

This thing called wine

Just what is this thing called wine, and why all the fuss over it?

What magic powers does it possess that move men to write soulful poetry, to form semi-secret wine cults and even designate Bacchus as its own personal god? What madness prompts otherwise sensible adults to attach a string of silly adjectives to a glass of fermented grape juice and treat it with theatrical reverence?

Try to imagine someone holding a glass of beer up to the light, swirling it, taking a sip and then saying, solemnly: "It lumbers rather than dances. It's of marginal quality for a beer of this pedigree, but some may find its funkiness appealing."

Rather foolish, don't you think?

Such a description was used—in all seriousness—by a wine writer after tasting a Corton-Charlemagne white from Burgundy.

Silly? Yes, but harmless. Let them love their wine. Certainly, it's better to worship wine than weapons. Wine has been known to cure writer's block (which we're proving at this very moment) and free the artist's soul. A chilled bottle of bubbly and a rumpled bed have patched up more lovers' quarrels than all the world's assembled marriage counselors.

A few sips from a glass will calm the troubled mind, settle the stomach and bring a measure of contentment to the spirit. It also is well established, of course, that too many glasses will trouble the mind, capsize the stomach and decimate the spirit.

So wine is fine, when used in moderation. But, getting back on track, just what is it and where did it come from?

That simple glass of wine you hold is hardly simple. A typical table wine is about eighty-five percent water and twelve percent ethyl alcohol (or ethanol), plus a trace of sulfites and tartaric acid. About 400 other components create a specific wine's color, aroma and flavor.

> *A chilled bottle of bubbly and a rumpled bed have patched up more lovers' quarrels than all the world's marriage counselors.*

Scientists don't even yet know what some of them are, or what they do. In fact, wine is among the most complex of all beverages.

The essence of the grape—particularly red—also contains tannin. That's the source of most of its astringency. Tannin lurks in the skins and seeds—and in stems and leaves which, hopefully, aren't floating around in the fermentation vats. You probably know that—with a few exceptions—most grape juice is white or pale yellow, even that squeezed from red grapes. Most coloration comes from the skins, which are left with the juice of red grapes during fermentation. Thus, both tannin and color pigments are leached into the wine.

Tannin is an antioxidant, a word you hear frequently in medical circles these days. This is an agent that prevents oxidation, the action of oxygen combining with other matter to form a new substance. Examples of oxidation are rusting (iron to iron oxide), silver tarnishing (silver to silver sulfide) and the conversion of wine to vinegar. Now, scientists believe that cholesterol oxidizes in the blood, causing it to settle onto arterial walls. The antioxidant qualities of the tannin in red wine may be a key to the prevention of heart disease. Much more on that in Part II.

Back to wine's components. If it's sweet, it contains a certain measure of residual sugar. This exists naturally in grapes in the form of fructose and glucose. They occur in about equal amounts, although fructose is considerably sweeter. Both are highly soluble sugars which, in the presence of yeast, are easily fermented into ethyl alcohol and carbon dioxide. In most other fruits, carbohydrates are stored either as less soluble sucrose or as starch; they have to be coaxed into fermenting.

Grapes have the highest sugar level of any fruit. They're perfect little fermentation factories, since wild yeast adheres to a sticky white coating on their skins. Step on a grape, let the yeast crawl into the juice, and wine-making begins. Originally, wine was made simply by stomping grapes and letting the natural yeast ferment the juice. Today, sulfur dioxide is added to kill the unpredictable wild yeast, then a cultured yeast is added to the juice to start fermentation.

A world in ferment

"God loves fermentation just as dearly as he does vegetation," wrote Ralph Waldo Emerson.

Indeed, that's what the wine business is all about: introducing yeast to grape juice, letting it ferment and bottling the results. Since you were interested enough to purchase this book (or, hopefully, you *intend* to purchase it), you probably know how wine is made. All that business about the grapes being fed into a stemmer-crusher to be mashed into a pulpy juice called "must," fermented, clarified, aged and cellared.

Perhaps more appealing for the wine curious is to learn precisely what's happening in that fermentation vat, where the just-squeezed juice is gurgling and burbling happily like an amiable witch's brew.

Fermentation is the conversion of one molecule of simple sugar into two molecules of ethanol and two molecules of carbon dioxide. It's the release of carbon dioxide that causes the bubbling. The catalyst, of course, is yeast, a member of the *thallophyte* family that includes lichens, algae and fungi. More specifically, it's a yeast enzyme called *zymase* that begins the fermentation process. When yeast comes into contact with a substance rich in soluble sugar, it begins consuming it to obtain growth energy. The process is similar to the way our bodies "burn" carbohydrates for energy, converting them to lactic acid in the muscles.

Unlike higher life forms, yeast doesn't require oxygen for this process. Indeed, winemakers discourage its presence, since oxidation causes a browning of the wine by converting ethanol into acetic acid, or vinegar. Certainly, you've tasted wines that have "turned" and become suitable only for salad dressing.

The process of fermentation has fascinated scientists for centuries. This "cold boiling" during the making of wine was one of mankind's first clinical observations.

The process of fermentation has fascinated scientists for centuries.

It laid the foundations for biochemistry and microbiology. The root words for yeast are believed to be Greek *zestos,* which became Anglo-Saxon *gist,* meaning "to boil," and *yasyati* in Sanskrit—"to seethe." To ferment literally means to boil and bubble while generating relatively little heat.

It was Dr. Louis Pasteur who discovered that fermentation was caused by the living organism of yeast, in 1857 during his studies at Lille, France. Noting that fermentation could occur without the presence of oxygen, he coined the terms "anaerobic" to define fermentation as life without air, and "aerobic" as respiration or life with air. He also was the first to confirm that oxygen was the culprit in spoiling wine, during and after fermentation.

When yeast cells metabolize sugar, they don't give a hoot about producing a good Zinfandel. To them, alcohol and carbon dioxide are useless byproducts. Their brief mission in life is to obtain enough energy to go forth and multiply.

Further, yeasts don't divide equally and form new cells the way most simple micro-organisms do. Parent cells send out buds that separate and become new cells. After launching a dozen or so offspring, the parent becomes old and dies. Accumulated dead yeast cells are part of the residue that must be clarified from wine.

In the production of sparkling wine, sugar syrup and yeast are added to an already-finished wine to start a second fermentation. This time, the carbon dioxide is retained to produce tiny bubbles. Later, the expired yeast cells are encouraged to accumulate in the neck of the inverted bottle, to be disgorged as a final step in the production.

One more note on the properties of yeast. Like most living things that absorb too much alcohol, it can become "pickled." If alcohol levels approach fifteen percent, yeast cells begin perishing in their own brew. Alcohol is a good preservative, so wines with eighteen percent or more alcoholic content won't spoil when exposed to oxygen. That unfinished bottle of sherry can stay around for months and still be drinkable.

A second kind of fermentation called malolactic can occur—either deliberately or accidentally—during wine production. This is the conversion of astringent malic acid to the rather bland lactic acid. Unlike yeast fermentation, it's a bacterial conversion.

Malic is the natural acid of "green" fruits, which is displaced as sugar increases during ripening. Every farmer knows that sunlight warming the chlorophyll of green plants activates the process of *photosynthesis*, by which sugars and other carbohydrates are produced. Indeed, it's the very essence of life on earth. In cooler climates where sugar build-up in grapes is limited, malolactic fermentation can help the wine, since it will soften harsh acidic edges. In warm weather areas that produce high-sugar and low-acid grapes—including most California winegrowing regions—it usually isn't beneficial. Excess malolactic fermentation makes wine insipid and flat. "Mousy" is a wine taster's term used to describe this condition. The same sulfur dioxide used to kill wild yeast will neutralize malic acid bacteria.

Assorted versions of this bacteria are abundant in nature, with intimidating names like *micrococcus, streptococcus, leuconostoc* and *lactobacillus*. Varieties of these critters are active in the production of cheese and sauerkraut. When your milk goes sour, it's the malic acid bacteria at work.

Alcohol: what it is and what it does

Basically, alcohol is a weak acid composed of a carbon atom cluster (called "saturated" carbon) attached to a *hydroxyl,* which is a grouping of one hydrogen and one oxygen atom. The chemical formula for ethyl alcohol is C_2H_5OH. Try to think of it as two saturated carbons linked to a fused hydrogen-oxygen atom. Alcohol is a close relative of glycerol, lactic acid, ether and even cholesterol.

Even those who profess to be abstainers take in a certain amount of alcohol. It's a naturally occurring substance in much that we consume. You'll find low-level amounts in most commercial fruit juices, and even in Coca-Cola. Further, the longer you keep a jug of apple, pineapple or orange juice around, the more the alcohol level increases.

The origin of the word is Arabic, which is interesting, since the Koran forbids the use of alcohol. Originally, however, it had other meanings. Scholars trace it to *kuhl* or *kohol,* referring to a fine cosmetic powder used to darken women's eyelids. From attention-getting makeup, *alkohol* or *alcool* eventually came to mean essence, or the most significant part of something. The first known link to wine came in the sixteenth century, when a Swiss-born physician and alchemist nicknamed "Paracelsus" referred to *alcool vini* as the most subtle part of wine. Three more centuries would pass before the word "alcohol" came into common use.

Incidentally, Paracelsus, who is credited with linking chemistry to medicine, was born Theophrastus Bombastus von Honenheim. He apparently took the name Paracelsus ("The successor of Celsus") to infer that he was superior to first century Latin physician Aulus Celsus. The original Celsus was author of *De Medicina,* regarded as the world's first medical book.

The word "spirit," in reference to alcoholic beverages, has Germanic roots. Ancients believed that drinking alcohol allowed one to communicate with the netherworld. (Some modern imbibers often succeed in doing the same thing.)

Alcohol's effects, while seeming rather complex, are actually simple. When you tip your glass, the alcohol is quickly absorbed into the bloodstream—about twenty percent through the stomach lining and the rest through the small intestine. This direct absorption without digestion is unique, and explains why alcohol's effects are felt so quickly.

Blood carries it to the brain, where it passes through that protective gray covering called the cortex. It quickly finds its way to the cerebrum, the upper part of the brain that controls your most complex and advanced functions. There, it acts as a depressant, inhibiting your mental signal system. One source described wine as a "muffler to the mind."

Alcohol has been mistakenly called a stimulant, since that first drink seems to make folks frisky. Actually, such high spirits occur because inhibitions are dulled and restraints are lifted from long-established behavioral patterns. If you drink too much, that urge to tell your boss to take a long walk off a short pier is not bravery, but loss of judgment.

Used in moderation, alcohol in wine does good things to the mind and body—easing tension, relaxing muscles, and reducing inhibitions just enough to encourage self-assurance and camaraderie.

The roots of wine

Scholars like to argue about which came first: beer or wine. Most say that beer was the first alcoholic beverage, since grain cultivation preceded grape growing. However, wine could have come first, since it can be made accidentally, while beer must be brewed.

"Some housewife probably left crushed grapes in a jar and found, a few days later, that an alcoholic product had been formed," according to Maynard A. Amerine and Vernon L. Singleton's *Wine: An Introduction for Americans.*

For decades, archeologists and wine historians felt that wine production dated from about 3500 B.C. Then in 1991, the discovery of wine stains on the shards of a pre-Bronze Age Sumerian jar pushed the date back even further. Fossilized grape seeds found in Stone Age middens suggest that folks may have been sipping wine 10,000 years ago. It is described as a sacrament in the earliest cuneiform writings, and the Bible mentions the essence of the grape more than five hundred times.

The Tigris-Euphrates Valley of Iran, Iraq and Turkey is generally regarded as the cradle of agriculture and therefore of civilization. Men and women began to "civilize" themselves when they were freed from the constant need to hunt and gather food. Agriculture enabled them to stay in one place, build permanent communities and contemplate such things as which wine to select for dinner. Around 3000 B.C., Noah parked his ark in the Tigris-Euphrates area, atop Turkey's Mount Ararat. According to Genesis 9:20-21, he "began to be a husbandman, and he planted a vineyard; and he drank of the wine and was drunken."

Thus, the Bible may be the first historical document to record a hangover.

The first prohibition movement probably started soon after, perhaps when a neighbor became angry at Noah's high spirits and loud singing. However, as Will Rogers pointed out five thousand years later: "Prohibitionists say that drinking is bad for you, but the Bible says that Noah made wine and drank it, and he lived to be 950 years old. Show me an abstainer who ever lived that long."

Noah's wine was pretty awful by today's standards. Since early societies had no knowledge of oxidation and no airtight containers, wine had to be consumed shortly after it was made, before it spoiled. Likely, it was unfiltered and rather turbid. (Somehow, I have this vision of Al Capp's Hairless Joe and Lonesome Polecat stirring up a vat of kickapoo joy juice.)

By the time of the Greek civilization, vintners developed methods of preventing spoilage and wine became an important export item. Anti-spoilage techniques added such offensive odors and flavors that wine was generally diluted with water prior to drinking. Among the "preservation" methods were adding heavy doses of herbs and smoking the wine to drive oxygen away. Romans added liquid resin and grapevine ash to the juice before it was fermented.

Some of today's stylized wines probably had their roots in crude production methods, or they were the results of accidents, surmises Justin Meyer in *Plain Talk about Fine Wine*. Retsina likely originated when clay jugs were patched with resin to keep them from leaking. Vermouth's herbs and juniper berries may have been early attempts at masking bad-tasting wine. The first sherries probably descended from oxidized white wines. Adding brandy to raise the alcohol level of dessert wines was—and still is—a method of preserving them. The grandest accident of all was the discovery of Champagne, when Benedictine monk Dom Pérignon's wine underwent a secondary fermentation. More on that at the end of Chapter Three.

The first detailed records of winemaking come from ancient Egypt. Tomb illustrations show workers stomping grapes with their feet, a practice that still continues in some areas. Egyptian hieroglyphics indicate that wine was reserved for priests and royalty; the ordinary pyramid-builders got beer.

Wine was an important part of Hebrew life and religion. Obviously, it was held in very high esteem. The Bible contains more than five hundred references to it, and Jesus equated red wine to his own blood. It remains a sacrament in many of the world's religious ceremonials; Catholic communion is a conspicuous example.

Greeks became skilled vintners, according to the writings of Homer, and wine was an important part of their daily lives. It was used to welcome traveling strangers, and it was an essential part of Grecian meals. It was the Greeks who conceived Dionysus or Bacchus, the god of wine, and wine was an important part of their religious ceremonies. Early writings also indicate that it was used medicinally, and it was applied to combat wounds in battle. This makes sense, since polyphenols in wine are powerful but short-lived germ killers.

> **Wine was reserved for Egyptian priests; ordinary pyramid builders got beer.**

Apparently, it still wasn't very good tasting. Often, Grecian wine was watered down and blended with herbs, spices, barley and—good grief—even feta.

By the time Rome rose to power, winemaking was an advanced skill, and possibly even an art. Author and philosopher Pliny may have been history's first true viticulturist, around the time of Christ. He cataloged grapes by color, ripening time and other characteristics. His writings reveal an intimate knowledge of climate conditions, soil and plant diseases.

Roman legions spread wines and vines throughout Europe. Viticulture was carried to France, thus beginning the great Gaelic love affair with the grape. Then in an historic reversal, Roman Emperor Probius outlawed wine grape growing in France. He may have felt that it was too competitive in Rome's export markets. Pliny's writings indicated the French wines were of poor quality, however. Could that have been—uh—sour grapes?

> *Many English, French and Spanish settlers, with the exception of teetotaling Protestants, brought their wine appetites to America.*

With the fall of the Roman Empire and the coming of the Dark Ages, wine production suffered. However, monasteries, needing wine for their religious rituals, kept the culture alive and probably even improved upon it. Further, the classic European varieties of today may have emerged during this period, developed from Middle Eastern vines brought back by the Crusaders. Most viticultural experts agree that noble varieties such as Cabernet Sauvignon and Chardonnay have their roots in the East. Some suggest that they're descended from a primeval Persian Muscat.

Coming to America

Many English, French and Spanish settlers, with the notable exception of teetotaling Protestants, brought their wine appetites to America. Wild grapes were abundant; indeed, early Norsemen who reached the coast of Canada called their landfall Vineland. However, the native American grape, *vitis labrusca*, was unsuited to wine production.

Thomas Jefferson, a whiz at writing constitutions, failed as a winemaker. He even tried importing European vines, but the weather around Monticello was too chilly. Later, a *labrusca* cross with European vines—perhaps accidentally—yielded varieties such as Concord and Catawba. Still in use, they produce a passable wine, if you like it on the sweet side.

America's true wine industry was born in California, where it remains rooted to this day. The Golden State's dry climate and balmy temperatures are responsible for nearly seventy-five percent of the country's domestic wine production. However, other states—particularly Washington, Oregon and New York—are increasing their wine output and winning some impressive awards. California also produces ninety percent of our table grapes and *all* of our raisins. Not surprisingly, Californians are among America's leading wine consumers, drinking nearly double the national average— about four gallons per capita compared with just over two in the rest of the country.

Every school kid knows that the state's settlement began when a gimpy legged padre named Junipero Serra started the first Spanish mission in San Diego in 1769. A surprising number of wine enthusiasts, and even many historians, think he planted the first grape vines there, thus giving birth to an industry. Some history books even provide detailed accounts of him sticking his precious vines into the ground—carried overland from Baja California—teaching the Indians to cultivate them and celebrating the first crush.

Not so, say scrupulous scholars. If the good padre brought European vines via Mexico, they weren't planted in San Diego. Or at least, they didn't survive. Twelve years after he arrived, he wrote: "I hope...the corn prospers and that the grape vines are living and thriving, for this lack of altar wine is becoming unbearable." He penned that letter from Mission Carmel near Monterey, not from San Diego. The first written evidence of the planting of a California vineyard was at Mission San Juan Capistrano north of San Diego, in the spring of 1779. Another document indicates that wine was made there in 1782, which would have been possible from three-year-old vines.

Eventually, vineyards thrived at most of the missions, and the padres did indeed launch California's wine industry. They used a *vitis vinifera* variety from Mexico that became known as the Mission grape. It probably was a cousin, perhaps a sister, to the *criolla*, still common in Mexico and South America. Of high sugar content, it yields a rather sweet wine, suitable for altar rituals but not for beef *bourguignon*. Records show that priests blended it with brandy to create a powerful padre cocktail which they called Angelica. Indeed, a few sips of this might put one—spiritually, at least—in communication with angels.

America's commercial wine production began, not in the famous valleys of Napa or Sonoma, but in Los Angeles. In fact, that sprawling community was once called "The City of Vineyards." The state's first commercially successful winemaker was Jean Louis Vignes, a French cooper from Bordeaux. He arrived in Monterey by ship in 1831 and adjourned to L.A. There, he started a cooperage and soon made enough money to plant vineyards; he ultimately established a major winemaking operation. History records that he was the first to import European grapes. Equally important, he's credited with planting some of the first orange trees in the state.

America's commercial wine production began not in the famous valleys of Napa or Sonoma, but in Los Angeles.

Vignes sold his orange and wine estate in 1855 to his nephews, Pierre and Jean Louis Sansevain, who had joined him from Bordeaux. They became the state's leading wine merchants and established its first commercial sparkling wine operation. Then in 1862, the brothers quit their business and California's pioneer vineyards eventually disappeared under spreading Los Angeles suburbs.

While not the first, Sonoma was the most important early seat of the state's wine industry. The story involves an unlikely pair—an energetic young Mexican lieutenant and a flamboyant Hungarian count of questionable lineage.

In the years following Father Serra's arrival, the missions had become vast agricultural empires, governed by the padres and worked by Indians who had been converted to Christianity—often unwillingly. Mexico won its independence from Spain in the 1820s and, some years later, it decommissioned the missions. The landholdings were parceled out to favored soldiers and politicians. Later, many Americans gained access to vast acreages by marrying into Mexican families.

Lieutenant Mariano Guadalupe Vallejo was sent to the northernmost mission, San Francisco Solano in present-day Sonoma, to oversee its dissolution. The ambitious young officer established a military garrison and laid out a townsite. A good politician, he quickly attained the rank of military *commandante* of all northern California. And he picked up thousands of acres in Mexican land grants. The assertive Vallejo soon became a major wine producer.

The man from Hungary

Enter the visionary gentleman of dubious lineage. Agoston Haraszthy (*Har-RAS-they*) arrived in Sonoma in 1856, met General Vallejo and purchased land to start a vineyard. He had come to America in 1840, fleeing his native Hungary after choosing the losing side of a revolution. He was variously known as Colonel Haraszthy or Count Haraszthy, although the source of his military title is vague.

He certainly was an ambitious fellow, and a gadabout promoter. In the sixteen years since touching American soil, he had founded the town of Sauk City, Wisconsin, crossed by wagon train to San Diego, dabbled in real estate, become a state assemblyman and later director of the U.S. Mint in San Francisco. He had attempted to raise wine grapes in Wisconsin, San Diego, San Francisco and San Mateo before finally finding the proper land and climate in Sonoma. The count and General Vallejo became fast friends. Two Haraszthy sons, in fact, married two Vallejo daughters and some of their descendants still live in the Sonoma area.

Haraszthy's Buena Vista Farm became the most prosperous wine empire in America, and he lived regally in a Pompeiian villa cresting a knoll above his vineyards. His greatest contribution to California viticulture was the importation of hundreds of thousands of premium European grape cuttings. He was commissioned by Governor William Downey to collect cuttings and wine knowledge to improve the state's industry. However, by the time he returned from Europe, Downey was out of office and the new administration refused to pay Haraszthy's expense account. The count distributed his cuttings throughout the state, selling them to defray his costs. Thus, perhaps by default, he earned the title of father of California viticulture.

The free-wheeling count's departure was appropriately bizarre. In 1868, restless for a new challenge, he went to Nicaragua to start a sugar cane plantation. Attempting to cross a stream one day, he fell into the water and vanished. Apparently, he was devoured by alligators.

Hard times for the grape

The young wine industry had to struggle during its formative years. Over-production and the depression of the 1870s dropped prices to ten cents a gallon. Then the industry was nearly ruined—both here and in Europe— by the invasion of *phylloxera,* a louse that destroys grapevine roots. It was an American louse but it hadn't been a problem here, since native grapes were resistant to its attack. Then, infected cuttings were shipped from New England to Europe, and later the bug made its way to California, where it attacked the new industry's European vines.

In 1880, the state legislature directed the University of California at Berkeley to establish a department of viticulture and enology. Its mission was to study phylloxera and other plant diseases affecting the wine industry. Later, it was expanded to include all phases of grape growing and wine production. However, Berkeley's chilly hills weren't suited to grape cultivation. In 1905, a field station was located near the small town of Davis, just west of Sacramento. From this has emerged the Davis campus of the University of California, one of the world's leading wine study institutions. It's also a major educational center with 100 undergraduate and eighty graduate programs in a variety of fields, plus schools of law and medicine. Davis is the largest of the state's university campuses, covering 5,200 acres, and it's third largest in enrollment. A second important California "wine campus" is at Fresno State University, in the heart of the large San Joaquin Valley grape and wine production region.

Toward the end of the nineteenth century, scientists finally found the solution to the phylloxera crisis. Both in Europe and California, the vulnerable European vines were grafted onto resistant American root stock. The wine industry was saved. For the moment, at least.

Then on January 16, 1920, passage of the infamous Volstead Act further brutalized the business, which was still recovering from the expense of battling phylloxera. We know it as Prohibition, with a capital "P." Repeal, with a capital "R," came on December 5, 1933, when Utah became the thirty-sixth state to ratify the Twenty-First Amendment to the Constitution, providing the necessary two-thirds majority. (There is historic irony here, since Utah is populated mostly with Mormons, who are tee-totalers.)

During that long dry spell, wineries struggled mightily, and two out of three closed. The rest survived by making sacramental wines and by selling grapes, since home winemaking was still legal. Particularly popular was a product with the wonderful name of Vine-Glo. It was a barrel of grape juice, complete with instructions for converting it to wine. Another product, a brick of compressed grape pomace, could be dissolved in water to create grape juice. A warning label stated:

Sorry, Elliott Ness, but the term "bootlegging" didn't originate with Prohibition.

This beverage should be consumed within five days; otherwise it might ferment and become alcoholic.

Since hard liquor couldn't be produced legally during Prohibition, that segment of the beverage industry went underground. Illegal stills and bootlegging became popular pastimes. (Sorry, Elliott Ness, but the term "bootlegging" didn't originate with Prohibition. It has been traced to the 1850s, when some puritan communities outlawed booze. Rum-runners smuggled thin, flat whisky flasks in their tall boots.)

The wine industry recovered slowly after Repeal. Thousands of acres of premium vines had been replaced with mediocre grapes better suited to the production of Vine-Glo and wine bricks. Many Americans had gotten out of the habit of enjoying wine, and the country was in the middle of the Depression. In 1934, several growers led by Napa's Louis Martini formed the Wine Institute to improve the quality of wine and promote its use. It's still the industry's leading voice.

World War II brought some financial respite to vintners. European wines were no longer available and the price of American wine grapes went from $15 to $50 a ton. However a shortage of labor, containers and rail cars retarded production. The industry didn't really get back on its feet until the decade of the Fifties.

By the Seventies, it had become fashionable to serve wine with dinner and America's winemakers were off and running, particularly in California. Since then, the number of wineries in the state has quadrupled from about 200 to more than 800. Grape growing and winemaking today are among California's leading agricultural industries, producing nearly $5 billion in revenue a year.

However, all is not rosy in the land of rosé. Followers of the Puritan ethic, still clutching their straight-laced heritage from Plymouth Rock, regard all alcohol as Demon Rum. And despite overwhelming evidence to the contrary, some health advocates still insist that wine is not good for you. Government agencies decided that—if wine is sinful or bad for your health—it should be taxed to raise the price and curtail drinking. And of course, warning labels are needed to discourage pregnant women from staying sloshed through their third trimester, and to advise people not to eat the lead foil wrappers.

Sales slumped during the peak of the anti-wine attacks from the 1980s into the early 1990s. However, they have recovered substantially in recent years, perhaps spurred by all the good news about wine and health. Total U.S. wine sales—from both domestic and foreign sources—topped 530 million gallons at the millennium, compared with 466 million gallons in 1991. Dollar value has gone up even faster, from $10.9 billion to more than $17 billion. This is primarily because of a shift from jug wines to premium varietals. In 1998, according to the Wine Institute, sales of better wines from California increased by fourteen percent while jug wine sales fell by three percent.

Americans are not only drinking more; they are drinking better.

Chapter two

KINDS OF WINES

What's behind those labels

This chapter is intended for two kinds of readers: those who don't know the difference between a Chardonnay and a Charbono, and those who want to learn more about that difference. For the most part, we'll be discussing wines that are enjoyed with food, which are simply—and universally—called table wines.

Taken collectively, wines of the world and their labels are very confusing. There is no common system for telling you what's in the bottle. Different countries have different methods of designating their wines— some by custom, some by law and some by whim.

Wines are identified by one of four methods:

1. The region in which they were grown; used primarily in France and to a lesser degree in Portugal, Italy and Germany. Thus, a red wine produced in France's famous Bordeaux region will simply be labeled as a "Bordeaux" or by a sub-district within that region. These countries also grade their wine by quality, from superior to *vin ordinare* (ordinary table wine).

2. The variety of the grape in the bottle, used primarily in California, most other American wine producing states and many other countries. By some tradition whose source escapes us, the word "varietal" is almost universally used, instead of "variety." They mean the same thing. In most states, laws govern how much wine of a specific grape must be in a bottle before it can be labeled as a varietal.

3. A *generic* description of what's inside, such as America's practice of calling anything red "burgundy" and anything white "chablis." This irks the French to no end, since Burgundy and Chablis are premium wine-producing areas. The quality of wines from these regions is taken very seriously in *La Belle France.* (Few premium wine producers in America use these generic terms, although many of the jug wine makers still follow this practice.)

4. *Proprietary* names, which are made-up brand names with no reference to anything, except possibly the advertising department's imagination. Gallo's infamous Thunderbird is a proprietary name, as is Blue Nun from Germany.

California and most other states do not grade their wines by quality. However, quality is certainly implied by the use of varietal or generic labels. Individual vintners may use more than one labeling method. Some large producers will sell you a "varietal" (Chardonnay), a "generic" (South Forty Burgundy) and a "proprietary" (Aunt Martha's Recipe Red) from the same shelf.

If you like a specific type of wine, it's important to know what variety of grape is in the bottle, since about ninety percent of a wine's character comes from its native juice. The remaining ten percent can be attributed to cellar handling, fermentation methods and aging. A bottle labeled California Burgundy, New York Chablis, or red or white table wine tells you nothing. However, if it says Amador County Zinfandel and you recall that this region of California's Sierra Nevada foothills produces a great Zin, then you have some direction.

This is the intent of this chapter—to describe the characteristics of various varietals and direct you to them. We list only the most popular wines produced in America. There are hundreds of other varieties in this country and worldwide.

Appellation: It's not a Virginia coal miner

Although much of what we say in this book refers to California and other American wines, we will briefly review the French wine label, since it both mystifies and confuses novice and even some intermediate enthusiasts. Besides, how can one possibly ignore the French in a book about wine? They produce more and—in most years—drink more wine than anyone else in the world. (If you study world wine statistics, you note that—year to year—the French and Italians seem to be engaged in a per capita drinking contest.)

> *Year-to-year, the French and Italians seem to be engaged in a per capita drinking contest.*

Further, most of the classic wine varieties that we drink and love originated in France. The list reads like a vintner's honor roll: Cabernet Sauvignon, Chardonnay, Pinot Noir, Merlot, Sauvignon Blanc and Chenin Blanc. Ironically, you rarely see these names on a French wine bottle, because of their labeling customs.

We mentioned in Chapter One that the early French became so adept at wine production it made their Roman conquerors jealous, thus creating the world's first wine snobs. Through centuries of winemaking, the French came to an obvious conclusion: particular varieties did best in certain soil and climatic conditions. From this emerged the practice of growing specific types in specific regions, and labeling the wines accordingly. This became known as *appellation d'origine,* literally the place of origin.

In 1891, most European countries signed a treaty in Lisbon, agreeing to honor one another's *appellations d'origine.* They would not use regional names on their labels unless the wine came from that area. Then in 1935, the French government went a step further, designating two levels of premium wine-producing areas and limiting the types of wine grapes that could be grown there. These were *Appellation Contrôlée* for the most outstanding wines and *Vins Delimites de Qualité Superiéure,* or V.D.Q.S. for the next highest level. If neither of these terms appear on a French label, you can bet it's jug wine.

Typical regions of *Appellation Contrôlée* are Bordeaux, Burgundy, Chablis, Beaujolais and Champagne. Within these are sub-districts; it is the smaller region's name that appears on the labels of most premium wines. The French take all this very seriously. (But then, the French take *anything* connected with wine very seriously.) Stiff fines and even jail sentences have been imposed against French winemakers caught violating the labeling laws.

Many countries, including ours, were not signatories to that treaty of Lisbon. To a good number of Americans, unwashed in wine knowledge, burgundy is red wine, chablis is white and Champagne is something with bubbles in it. However, many California winemakers avoid the use of these terms, out of courtesy to their French brethren. Some states, like Oregon, actually forbid their use.

So what does it all mean when you fetch a bottle of Château Haut-Brion from the shelf? It means that you're probably going to spend a lot of money, for this is one of the better wines of Bordeaux. However, the label doesn't tell you that. It will read *Premiere grand cru classé* (meaning it's good stuff), and *Appellation Graves Contrôlée*. This tells you it's from Graves, and you're expected to know that it's in the Bordeaux wine producing district.

We prefer the California labeling system. Both by law and custom, you know what wine you're getting.

What you don't learn from the label is the specific kind of wine that lurks inside. Red Bordeaux wines can be a blend of Cabernet Sauvignon, Merlot, Cabernet Franc, Malbec, Petit Verdod and/or Carmenere. You won't know the wine's alcoholic content, and a French label certainly won't tell you that the wine contains sulfites.

Therein lies an interesting irony in the French appellation system. Since several different varieties legally can be grown within each district, you don't know what grapes were used. Regulations in America decree that a wine labeled Cabernet Sauvignon must contain a high percentage of that variety—generally about seventy-five to ninety, depending on the state. So which is more important? To know that you're getting a blend of reds from a specific French château, or to know that you're getting wine that's mostly Cabernet Sauvignon? The French like their system because vintners can use their blending skills to create the best wines from the types of grapes that can be grown within their district.

We prefer the California system. By law and custom, you know what wine you're getting, unless it's a generic or proprietary brand. The label also tells you where it was made and bottled, its alcohol content and, in some cases, what vineyard it came from. Our sample wine label on the next page explains all of this in detail.

Most states now have appellation designations, called Approved Viticultural Areas (AVAs). Regulations don't dictate what grapes can be grown in these areas. However, they do require that eighty-five percent of the wine be from a specific AVA if it's listed on the label. If you happen to be fond of Zinfandel from the Shenandoah Valley, the label will tell you that's precisely what you're getting.

To shop intelligently for French wines, you need an encyclopedic knowledge of what châteaux are in which sub-district of what Appellation Contrôlée and how cooperative the weather was that year. If you like things *au natural*, you also may want to know whether the wine had to be ameliorated that year. That's a fancy term for adding sugar to the "must" (juice) when natural sugar levels aren't high enough. This practice is permitted in France and most other European countries. It's illegal in most American wine-producing states.

A final point in our brief French wine primer. France's wine producing areas have less predictable weather than most of those in America, and great vintage years are infrequent. While a late rain or early frost can damage some U.S. vineyards, the climate is relatively stable year-to-year in most American wine producing areas. It's not as critical to seek out a "great vintage" in an American wine.

To be fair, some of the world's grandest wines are those rare, great ones from France. Of course, a French *vin superiéure* will cost you dearly.

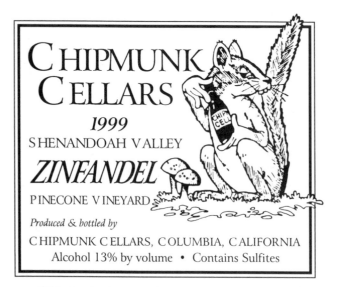

CHIPMUNK CELLARS

1999

SHENANDOAH VALLEY

ZINFANDEL

PINECONE VINEYARD

Produced & bottled by

CHIPMUNK CELLARS, COLUMBIA, CALIFORNIA

Alcohol 13% by volume • Contains Sulfites

1999: A wine can be vintage dated only if 95% of the grapes were crushed in that year.

Estate Bottled means that all the grapes used in the wine came from vineyards owned or controlled by the winery.

Shenandoah Valley is an appellation or Approved Viticultural Area (AVA), an officially designated growing region; 85% of the grapes must be from that area.

Zinfandel: A varietal name can be used only if at least 75% of the wine came from that grape.

Pinecone Vineyard is a "designated vineyard." To be listed, at least 95% of the grapes must have come from that vineyard, which must be located in an AVA.

Produced and bottled indicates that at least 75% of the grapes were fermented by the bottling winery. "Made and bottled" requires that only 10% of the grapes be fermented by that winery. Such terms as "Vinted and bottled" or "Cellared and bottled" are non-specific. They don't require the bottler to have produced any of the wine.

Alcohol 13% by volume: This can vary 1.5% either way. To be sold as a table wine, the alcohol content must be between 7 and 14 percent.

Contains sulfites: This statement is required on American wine labels if sulfite content exceeds 10 parts per million. It does in most wines. Some sulfites occur naturally in wine and most other foods; additional small amounts may be added to prevent spoilage.

A view of the varietals

If you've traveled in Europe, you'll note a major difference between most American vintners and those on the Continent. Individual European winemakers, either by law (as in France) or by custom, produce only one or two varieties of wine. You'll find different grades from similar blends of grapes, from superior to *vin ordinaire,* but not several different types of wines.

The idea of walking into a tasting room and sampling four or five varietals, plus a dessert wine and maybe even a sparkling wine, would be very foreign to foreign wine enthusiasts.

We Americans, perhaps spoiled by a supermarket mentality, seem to require a lot of choices. At most domestic wineries, you'll generally find a good selection of both reds and whites. Of course, because of climatic variations, some areas specialize in specific varietals, and we'll get into these in detail in the next chapter.

To help you choose among the many wines available, we present a list of varietals commonly produced by U.S. wineries. We reveal their original *appellations d'origine,* and tell you what to expect from them. Since California produces more than seventy-five percent of America's wines, we'll focus primarily on that state. However, we'll mention the three other major U.S. wine producing regions as well—New York, Washington and Oregon.

WHITE VARIETALS

Chardonnay (shar-doe-NAY) ● Regarded as the queen of whites, Chardonnay is a lush, soft and full-flavored wine whose color may range from straw to rich golden. The best will have a subtle nut-like flavor lurking behind the rich taste of fruit; a hint of apple or peach is not uncommon. It's one of the few white wines that improves with aging. Some vintners age it in oak to add a hint of wood to its complex flavor. The wine is sometimes called Pinot Chardonnay, although that reference is rare these days. Originating in France, it is the great white of the Burgundy and Chablis viticultural areas. It's also one of the two classic varietals use in the production of sparkling wine; the other is Pinot Noir.

WHERE TO FIND IT: Chardonnay grows best in cool coastal climates, such as California's Carneros region, a shallow basin where the Sonoma and Napa valleys merge above San Francisco Bay. It also does well in the slopes above the Napa Valley, northern Sonoma County and Southern Mendocino County. The Livermore Valley southeast of San Francisco is an excellent Chardonnay venue, although suburban sprawl is crowding out many of the vineyards. Some are retreating to the cool valleys of the Central Coast around San Luis Obispo, and in Temecula northeast of San Diego, where Chards are doing quite well. Elsewhere in America, you'll find good Chardonnays in New York's Long Island and Finger Lakes districts; Oregon's Willamette, Umpqua and Rogue River valleys; and western Washington, plus the Walla Walla, Yakima and Columbia valleys and Spokane County.

DINING PARTNERS: Rich and complex, Chardonnay is the natural companion for fish, shellfish and lightly seasoned poultry (no buffalo wings, please). We also like it with mild Cantonese fare, and with white sauce pasta. A particularly rich and nutty Chardonnay goes well with a midafternoon snack of mild cheese and crackers.

Chenin Blanc (SHEN-nin blawn) • An exceptionally fruity wine, Chenin Blanc grows in a wide range of climates, although it does best in moderately cool areas. The hue ranges from straw colored to almost colorless. Chenin Blancs fermented completely dry can be excellent, still retaining their lush, fruity flavor with a nice acid balance. In France, the wine is sometimes called *Pineau de la Loire*, since it originated in the Loire Valley.

WHERE TO FIND IT: Napa Valley produces California's finest Chenin Blanc, with northern Sonoma County not far behind. It also enjoys the climates of Monterey County, the Central Coast and Temecula. In the hot San Joaquin Valley, it's used to add a bit of fruit to the jug wines produced there. While most American Chenin Blanc comes from California, small amount also are produced in Oregon's Willamette, Umpqua and Rogue valleys and Washington's Spokane County, and the Walla Walla, Yakima and Columbia valleys.

DINING PARTNERS: Since it may range from slightly sweet to dry, it mates well with mildly spicy to rather subtly flavored foods. A dry Chenin, with a touch of fruit and crisp acid finish, is a good accompaniment to steamed or sautéed fish.

Fumé Blanc *(FU-may blawn)* ● Literally meaning "white smoke," Fumé Blanc is another name for Sauvignon Blanc. In California, the name was first used by Robert Mondavi in 1971. He fermented a Sauvignon completely dry, reducing the typical fruity taste sufficiently that a subtle smoky flavor came through. Some refer to the taste as gunsmoke, or even "flinty," a reference to the aroma of a flintlock rifle after it has been fired. Properly handled, Fumé Blanc is a crisp, slightly herbaceous and nicely balanced wine ideal with subtly seasoned foods. (See specifics under Sauvignon Blanc.)

French Colombard *(CO-lawm-bahr)* ● An ordinary and rather sturdy white wine, it's known simply as Colombard or *Colombar* in the Cognac district of

The best way to become acquainted with the tastes of various wines is to go winery touring.

France, where it's principally grown. Suited to California's warmer San Joaquin Valley, it's popular as a blending grape, often winding up as generic Chablis. Several wineries began producing it as a varietal a couple of decades ago, particularly in Mendocino County, although its popularity has faded. It is generally fermented dry, producing an acidic, crisp and almost tart wine. The hue ranges from pale golden to nearly colorless.

WHERE TO FIND IT: The moderately warm climates of northern Sonoma and southern Mendocino are suited to Colombard and a few wineries there still bottle it. It's rarely found as a varietal outside of California, except in a handful of warm climate vineyard areas.

DINING PARTNERS: The crisp, dry flavor goes well with lightly spiced fish and shellfish and not-too-spicy pastas. It will clash with any acidic foods and it will be muffled by spicy dishes.

Gewürztraminer (Ge-wurts-tra-MEE-ner) or (Ge-voorts-tra-MEE-ner) ● This German wine with the funny name is one of our favorite whites, and one of the few whites suitable with rather rich foods. A good Gewürz is fruity and spicy in both taste and aroma, even when fermented dry. The name, in fact, means "spicy traminer" in German. Some versions have a perfumed essence. Technically, it's not a white grape, since the skin has a rather rosy color, which can be imparted in the juice if it's fermented skins-on. Sebastiani Vineyards does this, producing an appealingly rose colored wine labeled Eye of the Swan. It's much more spicy and full-flavored than many rosés, and superior to most of those bland white Zinfandels that ran amok a couple of decades ago.

WHERE TO FIND IT: This popular Traminer ranges widely in Napa, Sonoma, Mendocino and Monterey counties. You'll find it on many vintners' wine lists, from spicy northern Sonoma versions to drier Napa Valley types. New York's Finger Lakes, Long Island and Hudson Valley produce this wine, and it's popular in all three major Oregon vineyard areas, as well as Washington's Yakima Valley.

DINING PARTNERS: This is a fun dining companion, since its rich spiciness can keep pace with a variety of foods. Although sommeliers may sniff at the notion, it's a good wine to order when members of the dinner party have selected a wide assortment of entrées. It'll bridge the gap from fish in cream sauce to poultry to lightly seasoned pork. Keep it away from that filet of sole, however; you'll taste the wine but not the fish.

Gray Riesling (REES-ling) • Never mind what the label says; this isn't a German Riesling, but the *Chauché Gris* white wine of France. (Some say it's not even a Chauché, but a descendant of France's ordinary *Jura* jug white.) Light in color, it's a soft, rather gentle wine with more of a spicy than a fruity flavor. Connoisseurs regard it to be rather ordinary. Although it's native to France, it isn't considered worthy of appellation designation.

WHERE TO FIND IT: The Wente Brothers winery in the Livermore Valley was one of the early producers of this blue-collar varietal, and it's still a popular wine in that area. You'll find versions in most other cooler regions of California as well, such as southern Mendocino, Napa-Sonoma and Monterey County. It's rare as a varietal outside of California.

DINING PARTNERS: Its subtle spiciness goes well with lightly to moderately seasoned fish and shellfish, and perhaps softly seasoned poultry and pasta. Try it well chilled with a mild cheese and cracker snack, or as a summer afternoon sippin' wine.

Johannisberg Riesling • Sometimes called white Riesling or simply Riesling, this is the classic German white, often compared with France's Chardonnay in quality. Color can range from golden to pale yellow. Its lush flavor is a bit fruitier than Chardonnay, without the nut-like subtlety. Vintners either ferment it dry or leave just a tad of residual sugar. With a hint of sweetness, it's a good "starter wine" for the novice, since it's refreshingly fruity, without the acidic nip of drier whites.

WHERE TO FIND IT: This popular wine is available throughout most of the coastal areas of California, both north and south. Several Napa Valley and Sonoma Valley wineries produce fresh, fruity Rieslings. You'll also find it in northern Sonoma and southern Mendocino, the Livermore Valley, Monterey County and Temecula. Elsewhere in America, where it's usually just called Riesling, you'll find it in all three major New York vineyard areas, and throughout Oregon and Washington vinelands. With its affinity for cooler climates, it does quite well in these three states.

DINING PARTNERS: Like its French cousin Chardonnay, it can be a versatile food partner, since it ranges from slightly sweet to dry. With its nice balance of acid and fruit, even the drier versions will work with moderately seasoned fish and shellfish.

Sauvignon Blanc (SO-veen-yawn blawn)

● California's sunny coastal climate is ideal for this grape. In proper hands, it emerges as one of the state's better whites and it's invariably less expensive than Chardonnay. The flavor is complex and fruity, with a touch of spice and a crisp acid finish. It wasn't popular until Bob Mondavi fermented it dry to reveal its spicy complexity; see Fumé Blanc above. Versions with a touch of sweetness have a lush, soft flavor almost rich enough to be a dessert wine. The leading white wine in the Loire Valley and the Graves region of Bordeaux, it's often called Blanc-Fumé by the French.

WHERE TO FIND IT: Napa Valley is the stronghold of Sauvignon Blanc, although it's a regular member of vintners' lists in Sonoma, Mendocino, the Central Coast and Temecula. It also is produced in New York, primarily in the Hudson Valley and on Long Island, and in Oregon's Willamette Valley and Washington's Spokane County and the Walla Walla, Yakima and Columbia valleys.

DINING PARTNERS: This is another versatile white, sharing the same dining flexibility as Chardonnay and Riesling. Try it dry with mild fish and shellfish; slightly sweet versions work with saucy fish, poultry and pork.

Sémillon (SEM-ee-yawn)

● A native of southwestern France, Sémillon is flowery in taste and low in acid. Fermented dry, it can be refreshing but rather bland; some versions have a bitter finish. With a bit of residual sugar, it is a pleasant sipping wine. Color can range from golden to light straw. Because of its tendency to be off-balanced, it's often blended with other wines, particularly high-acid Sauvignon Blanc. In France, such a blend with some of the residual sugar intact produces the great sweet Sauternes.

WHERE TO FIND IT: Sémillon is not a popular wine in California. A few Napa, Sonoma and Mendocino wineries bottle a dry Sémillon and some slightly sweet versions. Livermore Valley also is a producer, and it's planted in the San Joaquin Valley as a blending grape. Since Sémillon likes warm weather, it's not common in the cooler New York and Washington vineyard areas. However, it's produced in Washington's warmer Yakima and Columbia valleys and Oregon's Willamette Valley. Some American vintners produce a sweet Sémillon and label it "Sauterne," stealing the French Sauternes appellation. However, American sauterne can be anything, generally referring only to a sweet white wine.

DINING PARTNERS: You'll not find Sémillon on a lot of wine lists, and if it does appear, ask the sommelier if it's dry or sweet. Dry versions, with their subtle flowery taste, can be pleasant with mild fish and shellfish; save the sweeter versions for dessert.

Those other whites • A few other varietals may appear on vintners' lists, although they are becoming increasingly rare. Perhaps taking a cue from Europe, most American wineries are shifting away from a department store mentality and paring down their selections. After all, why make a mediocre Sylvaner when you can produce an excellent Chenin Blanc? Some of the off-whites are hybrids, created by Dr. Harold P. Olmo, the legendary viticulturist at the University of California at Davis. His goal was to create prolific bearers that could withstand the San Joaquin Valley heat and still produce decent wines. The success has been conditional. Davis has produced some palatable hybrids, although few have sold as well as varietals. Most wineries that marketed varietal hybrids have since dropped them in favor of the classics, as part of the general downsizing of wine lists. The hybrids still grow, but most disappear into jug wines.

Among the Davis blends in production are **Emerald Riesling,** a soft, light bodied wine; **Flora,** a flowery wine that attempted to compete with the

Gewürztraminer; and **Symphony,** a fruity medium white that has found some success as a sparkling wine grape. Château DeBaun in northern Sonoma County is pursuing a serious Symphony sparkling wine program.

Other whites (not hybrids) you may encounter are **Sylvaner** (*sil-VAN-ner*) a wimpy version of Chenin Blanc; **Green Hungarian,** a once-popular and rather flaccid wine whose roots are obscure; and **Folle Blanche** (*fawl blawnch*), a quite drinkable crisp and dry white once popular at Napa Valley's Louis Martini Winery. **Muscat** is a sweet, prolific hot-weather grape, usually dark golden, used in a variety of sweet and dry wines. The rich, fruity and raisiny taste is unmistakable. In fact, it's often used as a raisin grape. Some California winemakers produce a sweet Muscat Canelli dessert wine and New York state creates some interesting medium to sweet Muscat wines.

Generically speaking ● As you wander through the world of wine, you'll encounter **chablis,** which has no meaning, as we mentioned above. Most vintners are dropping the name in favor of the more honest reference—white table wine. **Rhine,** like chablis, is a no-name creature, generally found only in the cheapest jugs and box wines. This vague imitation of rich German wines is usually sweeter than a generic chablis. **Riesling** is another name borrowed from the Germans and attached to a white jug wine. In the generic order of things, riesling is between chablis and Rhine in order of sweetness. **Sauterne** usually refers to a sweet white wine. If it borders on sticky sweet, a winery may call it haut (*au*) sauterne. Sémillon and Sauvignon Blanc often are used in the making of it, and sometimes Muscat for the sweeter versions.

RED VARIETALS

Barbera (*bar-BEAR-ra*) ● A good, sturdy red that can abide hot weather, Barbera often loses its identity as a jug wine. In fact, it's one of the world's most commonly planted reds. A few vintners—particularly those of Italian lineage such as Napa Valley's Martini, Sonoma Valley's Sebastiani, Northern Sonoma's Pedroncelli and Gilroy's Fortino—bottle it as a varietal.

Perhaps America's best Barbera comes from the Louis M. Martini Winery, where it has been bottled as a varietal since the 1930s. Michael Martini, grandson of the founder says their Barbera—which is fermented over the skins of Petite Sirah and Zinfandel and then blended with some of those wines—is one of their finest reds. The Zin and Sirah bring up the tannin level to produce a nicely balanced wine.

To call it a spaghetti wine would not be unfair, since it originated in the Piedmont area of northwestern Italy and its hearty flavor is a good companion to spicy red sauces. It isn't a subtle wine. A proper Barbera is rather fruity, tart and high in acid. It's almost always fermented dry.

WHERE TO FIND IT: Most of California's Barbera thrives in the hot San Joaquin Valley, where it vanishes into the jug and box wines of mass producers. It's bottled as a varietal in a few wineries of the Sonoma Valley, Napa and Southern Santa Clara. Barbera as a varietal is rare outside California, except in a few small warm-weather wine producing areas.

DINING PARTNERS: Mangiamo! If you can find a Barbera on an Italian menu, go for it. Do not confuse it with Chianti. This is a specific wine from specific regions of Italy—notably Tuscany. (However, the name chianti is used generically on California labels.) With its acidic nip and full flavor, Barbera will pair nicely with seasoned red meats, red pastas, wild game and hearty stews.

Cabernet Sauvignon *(CA-buhr-NAY so-veen-YAWN)* ● If Chardonnay is the queen mother of the whites, Cabernet Sauvignon is the patriarch of the reds. In *La Belle France* it is the prince of Bordeaux, the main component of those legendary wines of Médoc and Graves, the exquisitely overpriced product of Lafite Rothschild and other noble châteaux.

It prompts serious aficionados to dip deeply into their den of adjectives. They manage to find in a glass of Cabernet the flavors of sun-dried fruit, figs, assorted herbs and spices, black currents, plums, cherries and vanilla. Indeed, a good Cab is the most complex of all varietals, so wine smugs can hardly be blamed for getting carried away with their descriptions. One thing even a novice wine enthusiast can detect—which separates Cabernet from all the rest—is the subtle aroma and bite of chili peppers. This herbaceous flavor is the trademark of the royal red of France. When fermented slowly and on the skins, this dark cherry red wine carries a tannic bite and is best drunk after years of aging. It's often kept in oak for a year or more after fermentation to give it even more complexity, then bottle-aged. A mature Cabernet has a lush, warm, soft and mouth-filling flavor that can only be described as indescribable. Unless, of course, you're a wine smug with a pet list of adjectives.

With an abundance of Cabernet in production, many vintners market young, lighter versions and it's now common as a jug wine. However, except for that hint of chili peppers, it loses much of its subtlety. Zinfandel, we think, makes a better young jug red.

WHERE TO FIND IT: Where not? Preferring moderate to moderately warm weather, it's grown in virtually all of California's premium wine-producing regions. Cabs are labeled from southern Mendocino and northern Sonoma to the Gold Country foothills, from southern Santa Clara County to the Central Coast. The best still comes from the perfectly balanced climate of the Napa Valley, with the Sonoma Valley as a close rival. Outside California, you'll find some good Cabs in all three New York State regions, Oregon's Umpqua Valley and east of the Cascades in Washington.

DINING PARTNERS: Good Cabernet frequently suffers the impatience of its owners; too often, it is served too young. That tannic bite will stand up to the richest of foods, but it won't be a happy marriage. A properly aged and mellowed Cab works with a wide range of meat and game dishes. The younger, lighter versions are good with rabbit or seasoned chicken and duck.

Carignan (car-een-YAN) ● Often spelled "Carignane" in California, this *vin ordinaire* rivals Barbera as one of the world's most widely planted reds. It's a native of Spain and provides the basic jug wine for Spain and France. Uncounted tons are grown in California's San Joaquin Valley as a blending grape, since it is high yielding and produces a good, honest everyday wine.

WHERE TO FIND IT: The best place to find Carignan is in a jug labeled "California red." A few Northern Sonoma vintners—notably Simi in Healdsburg—have bottled it as a varietal, along with Fetzer in southern Mendocino and Thomas Kruse and Ernie Fortino in southern Santa Clara County.

DINING PARTNERS: If you find Carignan on a restaurant wine list, which isn't likely, regard it as you would any medium red. Pair it with red meats, stews, red pasta sauces and the like.

Gamay Beaujolais (ga-may bo-zho-LAY) ●
About three decades ago, August Sebastiani introduced the old French *nouveau* custom to America—serving a red wine within weeks of its harvest. The wine was Gamay Beaujolais, particularly suited to this tradition because of its light, berry-like flavor. A good young Gamay suggests raspberries, and can be very refreshing when drunk chilled. In France, it is the predominate wine of the Beaujolais district, adjacent to Burgundy. It is, in fact, the most popular wine in that country. Because of its light, fruity flavor, it's often used in America to produce rosé.

Some California vintners attempt to distinguish between Gamay and Gamay Beaujolais, although that distinction is vague. Clinically, Gamay is the grape of the Beaujolais district, and Gamay Beaujolais may be a "frail strain of Pinot Noir," say Bob Thompson and Hugh Johnson in *The California Wine Book*. The taste—light and berry-like—is indistinguishable between the two.

WHERE TO FIND IT: A cool climate grape, Gamay thrives side-by-side with Pinot Noir and can thus be found in many southern Mendocino, Sonoma, Napa, Monterey and Central Coast vineyards. Look to producers such as Pedroncelli and Sebastiani of Sonoma County, and Neibaum-Coppola (formerly Inglenook), Charles Krug and Robert Mondavi in the Napa Valley. It's uncommon as a varietal elsewhere in America.

DINING PARTNERS: This is a fun wine, a suitable compromise at a large dinner party when everyone has ordered a different dish. (An even better compromise, of course, is to order several different varieties of wine.) Running the Gamay gamut of suitable entrées, you'll find that it works with poultry, pork, ham, lamb, mild-flavored game dishes and even fish when it's served in a sauce of some sort. We always drink Gamay slightly chilled—about sixty degrees.

Grignolino *(grig-noh-LEE-noh)* ● This native of Italy's Piedmont district is rarely bottled as a varietal in America. It's similar to its Barbera cousin, although a bit more tannic.

WHERE TO FIND IT: In California, Heitz Cellars and Beringer of the Napa Valley and Gilroy's Ernie Fortino and Thomas Kruse are among the few bottlers of Grignolino. It's infrequently found outside the state.

DINING PARTNERS: Follow the same suggestions as for Barbera, although you'll find Grignolino to be a bit more nippy, perhaps too much so for milder dishes.

Merlot *(mehr-LOW)* ● An important companion grape to Cabernet in Bordeaux, Merlot enjoys significant stature among California, Oregon and Washington vintners. It was almost unknown in America as a varietal a few decades ago. This is a lush, soft wine with gently rounded edges and is thus ideal for blending down the harsh tannins of Cabernet. As a varietal, it is gentle on the palate, comparable to a good Pinot Noir or young Zinfandel. A serious wine taster would say it lacks body and depth, although it offers excellent fruit and a pleasing aroma.

WHERE TO FIND IT: America's best Merlots come from Oregon, notably from the Willamette and Umpqua Valleys. New York's Finger Lakes district and Washington's vinelands east of the Cascades produce excellent Merlots as well. In California, it's bottled by most Sonoma, Napa, southern Santa Clara and Central Coast wineries, and by a few Sierra foothill vintners.

DINING PARTNERS: This soft, often lush wine is appropriate for a mixed menu, providing proper accompaniment to red meats, game, seasoned poultry, pork, ham and red-sauce pastas.

Petite Sirah *(pe-TEET sih-RAH)* ● The first thing the wine smug will tell you is that Petite Sirah, a native of the Rhône region, should not be confused with the Syrah of Hermitage. That's technically true but not important, since both are rather nondescript, high-tannin grapes that produce a dark ruby, full bodied and rather peppery wine. We doubt if the most talented palate could distinguish one from the other. Although a carefully-tended Petite can be crafted into a tasty, full-bodied wine, much of it grown in California and elsewhere in the U.S. is used for blending, to add an exclamation point to softer reds.

WHERE TO FIND IT: Concannon Vineyards in the Livermore Valley was among California's first wineries to bottle Petite Sirah as a varietal. It's still one of its trademark wines—full bodied, yet with rounded edges. A few Napa and Sonoma vintners also bottle Petite, although it is a minor item for them. It's uncommon as a varietal elsewhere in America.

Pinot Noir *(PEE-no Nwahr)* ● Second only to Cabernet Sauvignon among the classic reds, Pinot Noir can be identified by a berry-like taste, which often is silkier and lighter than Cabernet. These characteristics are subtle, however. A rather temperamental little grape, the Pinot varies considerably from one growing region to another; it's often difficult for the most educated palate to identify.

A proper Pinot is—and this is a compliment, not an insult—a basically sound red wine, without strong varietal character. It is thus no surprise that "Burgundy"—the French home of the true Pinot Noir—became the generic term for red wine in America.

Pinots tend to be light in hue—brick is a good description—and other reds may be added to bring up more color. However, some vintners manage to obtain a properly ruby color with a long, slow fermentation on their skins.

Although they aren't related except in name, Pinot Noir and Pinot Chardonnay are the mated pair for most great sparkling wines, including the Champagnes of France.

WHERE TO FIND IT: Pinot Noir likes cool climes and Oregon rivals California as America's finest venue for this wine. Pinots from the Willamette Valley frequently win medals, even in competitions in France. California's Carneros region between Napa and Sonoma valleys produces excellent pinos as well. Southern Mendocino, Monterey County and the Central Coast also offer proper Pinot habitats. Washington's arid inland wine producing areas are a bit too warm for Pinot Noir, although it does well west of the Cascades. Notable Pinots also are produced in New York's Finger Lakes district.

DINING PARTNERS: Since it can vary from light to moderately hearty, Pinot Noir is among the most versatile of dinner wines, suitable for everything from seasoned poultry to meats to pastas in red sauces. Try it with game, rabbit, veal or pork.

Ruby Cabernet ● This was one of Dr. Olmo's first hybrid successes—a late 1940s cross between Cabernet Sauvignon and Carignan. He hoped to produce a Bordeaux-style grape that would bear more heavily than the Cabernet, and also withstand hotter temperatures. It almost worked. Ruby Cabernet is a suitable drinking wine, although it's Bordeaux characteristics are nearly indistinct.

WHERE TO FIND IT: It's rare outside California. Within the state, a few Lodi-area wineries once produced it as a varietal, although it's difficult to find a bottle labeled Ruby Cabernet on any shelf these days. Most of the grapes are grown in the Sacramento Valley south of Sacramento (including the Lodi district), and farther south in the San Joaquin Valley. Virtually all disappear into jug wines.

DINING PARTNERS: This basic red is a basic companion for most items on the red-meat, spaghetti and stew side of the menu.

Zinfandel ● We've saved our favorite wine for last, but only by the dictates of the alphabet. Zinfandel is society's *volkswein,* a true wine of the people. It is perhaps the most versatile grape on the planet and one of the most widely-planted in California. The Zinfandel berry can be used to produce highly drinkable jug wines, occasionally outstanding varietals, excellent ports and universally appealing rosés.

> *Zinfandel is sassy and lively on the palate, a wine to be enjoyed and not taken so seriously.*

A proper Zin is refreshingly berry-like, and medium in color and body, with just enough tannic nip to give it character. Young plants will produce soft Beaujolais-style reds; old vines yield full-bodied, complex wines rivaling an occasional Cabernet. Some wineries, notably Ravenswood of Sonoma Valley, David Bruce of

Santa Cruz and Renwood in the Sierra Nevada foothills, produce high-tannin Zins that can be aged for years.

We like to think of Zinfandel as "California's wine." Its origin was a mystery for decades and since no other region claimed it, why not us? Many wine writers credit Agoston Haraszthy with introducing it to California from Hungary. However, it was here before the good count arrived. The mystery was partially solved in 1967, when a plant pathologist from the U.S. Department of Agriculture discovered that southern Italy's Primitivo is Zin's clonal twin. No one knows how it got to America, although it was being grown as a New England table grape in the 1830s. It may have been transported to California in 1848 by one Captain F.W. Macondray of Massachusetts.

Author David Darlington devoted an entire book, *Angels' Visits,* to the grape and its origins. He suggests that Zinfandel is a more approachable wine than its nobler European ancestors. It's sassy and lively on the palate, a wine to be enjoyed and not taken so seriously. Those who venerate Cabernet and Chardonnay are regarded as wine *aficionados*. We Zinfandel enthusiasts are more of a cult.

WHERE TO FIND IT: As one of California's most widely planted grapes, suited to a broad climatic range, Zinfandel is produced by many wineries. Some of the better versions come from Northern Sonoma County (Pedroncelli, Dry Creek, Topolo and Lytton Springs), Sonoma Valley (Ravenswood, where Zin is a specialty) and the Napa Valley (notably Sutter Home, which started the white Zinfandel craze two decades ago). Several Gilroy area vintners and those around Paso Robles on the South Central Coast make fine Zins. The state's *primo* bottles come from the Gold Country; the sloping Sierra Nevada foothills provide perfect growing conditions for the mystery grape. Look for a Zin with an Amador or Calaveras county designation on the label. "California's wine" is found infrequently outside the state.

DINING PARTNERS: With its medium body and subtle berry-like taste, Zinfandel is a versatile dinner companion. Like Pinot Noir, it compliments most red meat dishes, veal, pork, rabbit, game, seasoned poultry and pastas with red sauces.

Those other reds • Here are some other minor luminaries among the ranks of reds which you may encounter on wine labels: **Charbono**, a full-bodied wine from Italy, occasionally bottled as a varietal in the Napa Valley and northern Sonoma; **Pinot St. George,** a medium-bodied red from France, now rare as a varietal; plus two full-bodied wines that are prevalent in Italy and slowly gaining popularity in California—**Nebbiolo** and **Sangiovese**. All of the above wines are rare outside of California; most other American wine-producing areas seem preoccupied with the more classic varietals.

Generically speaking • The word **burgundy** on an American wine label means only that it is red, as we established earlier. **Claret** is a term used mostly in England to define a red table wine. It's not to be belittled, however; an Englishman's Claret often is the best of the Bordeaux. **Chianti** is used on some American wine labels to describe a medium-bodied spaghetti wine, perhaps in a raffia-wrapped bottle. The juice inside may or may not have its roots in Italy. True Chianti comes from a specific Italian region, and Chianti Classico is one of that country's better wines. Some large California producers peddle a **vino rosso,** a slightly sweet table wine. To our thinking, it isn't suitable for table use, except possibly as a dessert topping.

THINKING PINK

Rosé isn't a varietal, but a method of making wine. In France, the word merely means "pink." Most rosés are made from red grapes by pulling the skins early during fermentation to leave a slight hue in the juice. Also, rosé can be produced merely by blending red and white wines, although this is rarely done in America.

Most serious enthusiasts regard pink wine as a poor compromise between red and white. Marketing strategies by some wineries suggest that rosé "goes with everything," which really means that it's not the ideal wine for anything. Diners intimidated by long wine lists often seek refuge in rosé. Traditionally, most pink wine has been made from Grenache, a sweet, high-yield grape from southern France. Although that nation has made some great rosés, most of that produced in America was considered rather ordinary.

Then in 1958, Sonoma County's Pedroncelli Winery produced a rosé made from high-quality Zinfandel grapes and labeled it "Zin Rosé." The raspberry-like complexity of Zinfandel produced a much more pleasing pink wine, and it began winning awards. Others followed, with names like Rosé of Cabernet, Rouge Noir and the notorious "white Zinfandel." Sebastiani Vineyards produces a pink Gewürztraminer called Eye of the Swan.

In the 1970s, wine writer Jerry Mead coined the term "blush wine" to describe a rosé produced at northern Sonoma County's Mill Creek Vineyards, and the floodgates were opened. Soon, Zinfandel Blush, Cabernet Blush, Pinot Blush and white Zinfandel were among America's best-selling wines. White Zin led the pack, particularly after Sutter Home Winery's Bob Trinchero got into the act. Buying up every loose grape he could find and mass-producing white Zinfandel, he practically cornered that market. In 1987, he sold 2.5 million cases, catapulting Sutter Home from one of Napa Valley's smallest wineries to one of its largest.

As the Twentieth Century came to a close, pink had begun to shrink, since the novelty had become as thin as the wine. Figures released in 1999 showed that national sales of blush wines (52.6 million cases) finished third behind whites (75 million cases) and reds (62.2 million).

DINING PARTNERS: Although a well-made Zin Rosé or Rosé of Cabernet can exhibit some character, we feel this thin, fruity wine is mostly suited to picnics and lazy summer afternoons on the front porch swing.

A BIT OF THE BUBBLY

Like rosé, Champagne is not a wine variety but a production method. In fact, the classic process for producing sparkling wine is called *méthode champenoise,* which involves seventeen different steps.

As discussed in the previous chapter, sparkling wine happens when a secondary fermentation is induced and the carbon dioxide bubbles are retained. In the classic method, yeast and a sugar syrup are added to bottles, which are then sealed, usually with stainless steel caps. Fermentation takes about two weeks, although the newly-forming sparkling wine stays in the bottle much longer—from six months to two years, while it matures and the yeast cells break down.

Then, in an operation called "riddling," the bottles are placed neck down in a rack and tilted at a sharp angle so the dead yeast cells settle into the neck. (In most modern wineries, a small plastic cup called a *bidule* is placed in the neck to collect the fallout.) Periodically, a "riddler" gives the bottles a quarter turn and sharp jolt to keep working the cells downward. A quick-handed riddler can spin 30,000 bottles a day. Some wineries do this mechanically with riddling racks that vibrate or tilt.

Next, in the disgorging operation, the neck is placed in an icy-cold brine solution to freeze the plug of yeast sediment; the cap is popped and the frozen plug pops out. Since a little wine is lost, the bottle is topped off with a *dosage* (rhymes with "garage"). This also establishes the dryness of the wine, based on the sweetness of the *dosage,* which is a blend of sugar syrup, white wine and sometimes a touch of brandy. (Without a *dosage*, sparkling wine would be completely dry, tart and not very tasty.)

Three other methods may be used to produce sparkling wine:

In the **transfer process**, the secondary fermentation and aging take place in the bottle. Then the wine is transferred to a pressure-sealed tank for filtering and returned to a bottle—not the original one—for corking. The fine print on the label will tell you whether the sparkling wine was "produced in *this* bottle" or "produced in *the* bottle."

Less expensive sparkling wines are made by the **Charmat process**, named for the French inventor of the method. Secondary fermentation occurs in a sealed tank, then the wine is filtered and bottled. The most knavish of the sparklers are produced simply by **carbon dioxide injection** into a tank of wine. Although Charmat production is common in America, carbon dioxide injection isn't.

Taste should tell you which bubbly was produced in a bottle, since its close quarters with the yeast imparts a crisp tang. Also, Charmat and injected sparklers aren't aged, and they often have a "grassy" flavor.

Most sparkling wine is white, even though the often-used Pinot Noir is a red grape. The skins are pulled almost immediately after the crush, leaving the juice nearly colorless. Other wines commonly used for sparklers are Chenin Blanc and French Colombard.

Driest of the sparkling wines is *brut*, followed by *sec*, *demi-sec* and *doux*. The latter two are definitely dessert wines, too sweet for the main course. In a wonderful contradiction, some American bottlers use the term "extra dry" to identify a wine that's sweeter than *brut*.

Pink champagne is simply a rosé that has been secondarily fermented, almost always by the bulk process. A few decades ago, Cold Duck and Sparkling Burgundy experienced brief waves of popularity. Tasting like fermented soda pop, they were popular with folks who also had Pepsi with *coquilles Saint-Jacques*. Should you wonder, "cold duck" comes from the German expression *kalte end*. It refers to leftover dinner wines which servants would pour together and drink during the clean-up. Having tasted Cold Duck, we find it to be a suitable name.

> *Cold Duck and Sparkling Burgundy were popular with folks who had Pepsi with coquilles Saint-Jacques.*

In California, most of the better sparkling wines come from the Napa and Sonoma valleys and the Carneros region between them. This is an ideal appellation for its principle ingredients, Chardonnay and Pinot Noir. Among wineries specializing in sparklers are Gloria Ferrer Champagne Caves and Domaine Carneros in the Carneros region, Domaine Chandon, Mumm Napa Valley and Larkmead Vineyards in the Napa Valley and the venerable Korbel Champagne Cellars in northern Sonoma County's Russian River Valley. You'll also find a few sparkling wine producers in most of the New York, Oregon and Washington wine-producing regions.

DINING PARTNERS: Clean, crisp and effervescent, a good sparkling wine is the universal drink for wine enthusiasts. Sip it with virtually any kind of food, from cheese and crackers to pepper steak. Its clean flavor won't mask the mildest of dishes, and its sparkle will stand up to spices and sauces.

Real Champagne is frankly French, accidentally discovered late in the sixteenth century by a Benedictine monk in Hautvillers, near Reims. The district of Champagne became one of France's first *appellations d'origine,* and most nations honor the French wish not to use the word generically. Many American producers follow suit, often referring to their products by pleasantly contrived names: "Blanc de Blanc" (white wine from white grapes) and "Blanc de Noir" (white from black, as in Pinot Noir). Others simply call it sparkling wine. It is *Sekt* in Germany, *Spumante* in Italy and *Espumante* in Spain and Portugal. The Russians tip their glass and say: *Shampanskoe!*

The night they invented Champagne sounds suspiciously contrived and theatrical, but it's a cute story, so we'll repeat it:

Dom Pérignon, who was cellarmaster for the Benedictine Abbey from 1668 until 1715, made some white wine, decided that fermentation had stopped, and bottled it. However, some yeast remained and it became active when the weather warmed the next spring. Padre Pérignon sampled his wine sometime later, his eyes lit up and he cried: "Come quickly. I am drinking stars!"

DESSERT WINES

California has only one truly native dessert wine, **Angelica,** produced by the padres from the mission grape, which had been brought up from Mexico. Records show that they drank it as a powerful blend of three-fourths sweet red wine and one-fourth brandy. No wonder the Indians had to do all the work!

Sonoma's Sebastiani Vineyards, one of the few still growing the old mission grape, bottles a sweet Angelica, but without the brandy. A few other wineries produce specialty dessert and appetizer wines from high-sugar grapes such as the Palomino, Tinta Madeira, Malvasia and Muscat. They appear on the shelves as **Muscat Frontignan, Madeira, Malvasia Bi-**

anca, **Black Muscat** and **Muscatel.** Another example is **Tokay,** an amber pink wine produced from the Flame Tokay grape of Hungarian origin. Few of these wines get much respect, since their high alcoholic content make them the drink of choice for derelicts who nip from bottles shrouded in paper sacks while huddled in urban doorways.

As we mentioned in Chapter One, sweet wines are produced by stopping fermentation before all the sugar is converted into alcohol. One of several methods may be employed, sometimes in combination: chilling or heating the wine to kill the yeast, filtering out the live yeast cells, or adding brandy, which elevates the alcohol content to pickle the yeast cells.

The most common desert wines have their roots in Spain and Portugal, and American versions are widely produced.

Sherry ● Generally made from the Palomino grape, sherry originated near the small town of Jerez (*Hair-ETH*), near Seville. "Sherry" comes from an Anglicized mispronunciation of the name.

In Spain, elegant sherries are made by an elaborate process. After the grapes are crushed and the juice is fermented, it is clarified, blended and then aged in 150-gallon casks to form a pale dry wine. It is later fortified to about fifteen to eighteen percent alcohol with brandy to prevent spoilage, and a special *flor* yeast is added. Named for

> *The most common desert wines have their roots in Spain and Portugal, and American versions are widely produced.*

the floral patterns that form on the surface, the yeast partially oxidizes the wine, giving it the rich caramel color and nutty taste associated with a fine sherry.

After more aging, the barrels are stacked in tiers, and wines of different vintages are drawn down from one barrel to another. In this *solera* process, young sherries are married with older wines through the years to gradually produce a uniform blend. Sherry is then drawn off from the lowest tier and bottled. *Solera* refers not to the sun but to *suelo,* meaning the floor or base. The *suelo* barrels are never completely emptied; they perpetually receive blends of younger wines from the upper tiers. Thus, a sherry from an ancient Spanish winery may contain wines from more than a hundred different vintages.

In America, the process is considerably less romantic. The fortified wine is simply heated and baked to achieve the caramelized appearance and taste. A rare few California wineries do use the complex *solera* racking process.

However, to get a truly magnificent sherry, you should turn to the source.

Port ● Another popular dessert wine named for its source, port comes from the Duoro Valley near Oporto in northern Portugal. Tinta Madeira and several other high-sugar grapes are used in its production. As with sherry, the alcohol content is elevated by the addition of brandy. Unlike the sherry process in which the initial wine is fermented dry, brandy is added in mid-fermentation to preserve much of the port's native sugar.

Virtually all ports have a rich, sweet taste while some sherries can be quite dry.

Thus, virtually all ports have a rich, sweet taste while some sherries can be quite dry. After brandy is added, Portuguese port is aged, sometimes for decades.

In America, the process is similar although ports are rarely aged. A few California wineries produce memorable ports, notably Richard Matranga's Sonora Wine and Port Works in the Gold Country, plus Andrew Quady and Ficklin, both near Madera in the San Joaquin Valley. (Madera's name is only coincidentally similar to Madeira, the wine often used in port production. *Madera* is Spanish for lumber, referring to a wooden flume that floated logs into the San Joaquin Valley from Sierra foothill forests after the California Gold Rush.) Zinfandel, by the way, is becoming a popular wine base for California ports.

APÉRITIFS

An apéritif is a beverage taken before a meal, be it a wine, cocktail or a shot of Jack Daniel's. *Apéritif* simply means appetizer in French. Conceivably, the word also could refer to smoked oysters or lemonade.

Among wines, dry sherry is the most popular apéritif. Dry sparkling wine also fills this role admirably. Fashionable apéritifs in Europe—but uncommon here—are vermouths and wine-based proprietary drinks such as Dubonnet, Pernod, Amer Picon and Compari.

We end this review of wine varieties with some interesting trivia. America produces four times as much sherry as Spain and ten times as much port as Portugal. That doesn't seem to concern the Spanish and Portuguese. These dessert varieties comprise only about two percent of their total wine production. Both nationalities drink about seven times more wine per capita than Americans, and each country produces more table wine than we do.

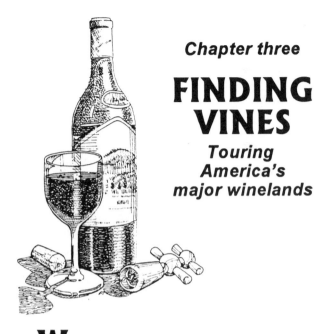

Chapter three

FINDING VINES

Touring America's major winelands

W inery touring has become a popular American pastime. Each year, millions head for the vineyards to enjoy the privilege of sampling wine at the source.

This ritual provides an obvious advantage: You can try before you buy. Many wineries, eager to sell their products at retail instead of wholesale prices, have added gift shops, picnic areas, even restaurants and other measures of ambiance to entice the touring crowd. Some of the newer wineries are designed specifically with tourism in mind. Many smaller ones rely entirely on visitors, selling their wines only at the source. In areas such as California's Napa Valley, winery touring and tasting has become a multi-million-dollar business. Some large wineries there attract more than 300,000 sippers a year.

When most people think of winery touring, California comes to mind. Indeed, as we noted earlier, the Golden State produces seventy-five percent of America's wine. However, forty other states have commercial wineries, even tropical Hawaii and arid Nevada.

This slim book will not attempt to guide you in detail through America's diverse vinelands. Other publications do a much better job. We will instead offer a brief look at the country's more popular wine producing areas. We'll tell you how they came to be and what kinds of wines you'll find there. We'll start with California's extensive vinelands, then visit those of the next three largest wine-producing states—New York, Washington and Oregon.

Winery touring tips

Before we begin, here are some tips to heighten the enjoyment of a trip to the wine country:

1. *Plan your route in advance* by picking up a winery guide, and set practical goals. (We list sources of winery guides later in this chapter.) Don't try to cover more than four or five wineries in a day. There is much to enjoy, to learn and to see in America's vinelands. Why rush through the wineries? Be selective.

2. *Limit the number of samples* you try at each winery, as well as the number of wineries you visit. We usually sip no more than four wine varieties per stop. If you taste too many wines, their differences will begin to blur. So will your vision. Save the urge to party until you're safely back home or in your hotel room, off the highway and close to the floor.

3. *Hit the wine country on weekdays*, if possible. This is particularly important for popular California wineries, which can become very congested on weekends. If you're limited to weekend visits, get an early start. It may go against your instincts to begin sipping at 10 a.m., but you're there to sample wines, not engage in social drinking. Most tasting rooms, even in the busy Napa Valley, are uncrowded in the morning. The crowds hit after lunch and build until closing time. In some smaller wine producing areas, however, tasting rooms may be open only on weekends, so check before you start out.

4. *Plan for a picnic*, since many wineries have picnic areas, often among the vines. Usually, you can find a deli nearby, and many tasting rooms also sell picnic fare. And don't be a plebeian; buy your picnic wine at the host winery.

5. *Tour wineries during the crush.* You can watch the proceedings and perhaps sample some of the grapes. At small wineries, you may even get to sip some "must," the freshly rendered juice. America's grape harvest ranges from late August through October, so check to see what's being picked where.

Sipping safely in the wine country

Overall, wine is involved in only two to three percent of alcohol-related traffic accidents. However, in a region busy with wineries that are giving away free samples, there might be a temptation to over-indulge.

Traffic safety officials have set reasonable limits for those who drink and then operate vehicles. Studies indicate that typical adults weighing 130 to 190 pounds should be able to drive safely if they limit themselves to one and a half ounces of alcohol over a two-hour period. Since table wine is about one-eighth alcohol, this translates to three four-ounce glasses of wine or twelve one-ounce "pours" or samples in a tasting room.

Using this figure, you could safely visit three wineries and try four wines at each over a two-hour period. If you purchase a bottle for a picnic, and you're the driver, don't fail to figure this into your quota. A 750-milliliter bottle of wine is 25.4 ounces, containing about three ounces of alcohol. If you and your partner share a bottle, that's *all* you should drink during a two-hour period if you're the driver.

Enough of this serious stuff. Let's go taste some wine.

CALIFORNIA

Ask many folks where California's wine country is located, and the answer likely will be: "the Napa and Sonoma valleys." Certainly, these are the most famous areas, yet they represent only the tip of the grape bin. In fact, a very small percentage of California wine comes from these two regions.

Wine grapes are grown in forty-five of the state's forty-eight counties. However, premium varietals—fussy about climate and soil conditions—are much more restricted. For the most part, they're limited to coastal valleys that get a good mix of sunshine, ocean breezes and cooling fogs. These areas account for less

California Wine Regions

Mendocino/Lake Counties
○Ukiah
Northern
Sonoma
County ○Santa Rosa
Sonoma ○ *Napa–Up Valley*
Sonoma ○ *Napa–Down*
Valley ○ Valley ○ *The Gold Country*
○Placerville
○Plymouth
Sacramento ○Murphys
○Columbia
○Livermore
San Francisco ○ *South Bay Areas*
○San Jose
Santa Clara County○SantalCruz
○Gilroy
Monterey ○ *Southern Santa Clara*
○Gonzales
Monterey County
○Paso Robles
○San Luis Obispo
South Central Coast
○Solvang
○Santa Barbara
● **Los Angeles**
○Riverside
Temecula✕ *Temecula Valley*
○Escondido
○San Diego

than fifteen percent of the state's total wine output, although they contain the great majority of its tasting rooms.

The rest of the state's wine comes from the vast vineyards of the hot and dry San Joaquin Valley of central California and the smaller Sacramento Valley to the north. Jointly, they form the state's 400-mile long Central Valley, once the bed of a giant inland sea. Incidentally, wine isn't the only thing produced in this huge valley. It's America's largest single agricultural area, producing an astounding forty percent of our total national food supply. Not surprisingly, California's is America's leading agricultural state.

But, back to the premium wine areas. A happy accident of topography provided ideal conditions for California's choicest grapes. Through the millennia, earthquakes rumpled the shoreline into a series of jumbled low hills, collectively called the Coast Range. Rivers carved shallow valleys, ranging from a few thousand yards to several miles wide. Warm water of the offshore Japanese current, mixing with cooler inshore water and the outflow of inland air combine to create almost perpetual condensation. Much of the time, a 2,000-foot-thick blanket of fog hangs offshore, to be drawn into coastal valleys as the inland air heats and rises. Then as the intruding chilly air is warmed, it dissipates and retreats.

It is this almost perpetual cycle that gives summer San Francisco visitors goosebumps. They step from their hotel rooms in shorts and halter tops in August, to be greeted by a chilling fog. Mark Twain once said the coldest winter he ever spent was a summer in San Francisco.

These conditions create a myriad of microclimates within coastal valleys, depending on their size, elevation and alignment. A wide variety of grapes can thrive within these pockets. Coastal fogs rarely reach into the Central Valley; thus its climate is hotter and drier during the growing season. Its infamous fogs come in winter, when the grapes are dormant.

A happy accident of topography provides ideal conditions for California's premium grapes.

In years past, most of California's better wines have been produced in vineyards near San Francisco Bay—Mendocino, Sonoma and Napa to the north and the Livermore and Santa Clara valleys south. Northern counties are still major producers, although south bay grapes are being squeezed out by the population crush of Silicon Valley. Vintners there have found new horizons, mostly in Monterey and Santa Cruz counties just to the south, and the South Central Coast between Monterey and Santa Barbara. One of the state's newest vineyard areas, dating back less than thirty years, is the Temecula Valley above San Diego.

The one exception to premium coastal valley vine-lands is the Sierra Nevada foothills of the California gold country. Here, sheltered valleys with higher elevations provide a wide range of suitable climate zones, particularly for fine red wines.

TO LEARN MORE: There is no shortage of books about California wineries. However, in all immodesty, we feel that the most comprehensive is our own *Best of the Wine Country*. Unlike most winery guides that focus on Napa and Sonoma, ours covers the entire state. It features nearly every tasting room in California that keeps regular hours, from Mendocino County to Temecula. The book also lists nearby restaurants, lodgings and other wine country attractions. It's available at book stores everywhere, and if it's not in stock, it can be ordered. Details are in the back of this book.

Mendocino & Lake counties

Overlooked by most wine country explorers, this bucolic landscape, thatched by oak groves and rimmed by pine-clad hills, is one of the state's more attractive regions. Southern Mendocino County has been creating wines for more than a century, but until recently, most of it was bulk production. However, one Charles Wetmore sailed off to the Paris Exposition of 1899 with some of his Mendocino wines and sailed back with *le grand prix*.

Tryfon Lolonis and Adolph Parducci were two other Mendocino wine pioneers. Greek immigrant Lolonis planted vineyards in the Redwood Valley in 1920; Italy's Parducci opened a Cloverdale winery in neighboring Sonoma County in 1916, then moved to Mendocino's Ukiah in 1931. A Lolonis descendant still makes wines and Parducci is the largest winery in Mendocino County.

Winemaking didn't become a serious growth industry until the early 1970s. Most growers sold the fruits of their labors to Sonoma County wineries. Then, realizing that Sonomans kept winning medals with Mendocino grapes, many began bottling their own.

Many of the area's wineries and vineyards are focused around Ukiah and a charming little hamlet to the south called Hopland. California's northernmost wineries are in the Redwood Valley north of Ukiah. Perhaps the most attractive area is the Anderson Valley, west toward the ocean along State Highway 128.

East of Ukiah, thinly populated Lake County is wrapped around Clear Lake, California's largest natural freshwater pond. It has barely enough residents to fill a football stadium—less than 60,000. This peaceful, bucolic land would be an island in time, ignored by the world outside, except that Clear Lake draws thousands of summer visitors. Several vineyards and a few wineries rim this cool pond.

Most wineries in the Mendocino-Lake County region are small; the folks pouring your wine may be the ones who made it. Anderson Valley is a good place to go touring, since half a dozen wineries line Highway 128. Also, several tasting rooms—detached from their wineries—are clustered in Hopland.

KINDS OF WINES: Mendocino is among the coolest of California's wine areas, particularly suited to Chardonnay, Chenin Blanc, Gewürztraminer, Sauvignon Blanc and other whites. Most vintners add a few reds to their mix as well. Inland Lake County is a bit warmer, offering a good balance of red and white wines.

TO LEARN MORE: For a *Lake County Wineries* map, contact the Lake County Grape Growers Association, 65 Soda Bay Road, Lakeport, CA 95453; (707) 263-0911. A *Mendocino Wine and Unwind* map and brochure is available from the Mendocino Winegrowers Alliance, P.O. Box 1409, Ukiah, CA 95482; (707) 468-9886 (WEB SITE: www.mendowine.com; E-MAIL: mwa@mendowine.com). For the *Anderson Valley Winegrowers* map: Anderson Valley Winegrowers Association, P.O. Box 63, Philo, CA 95466.

For tourist information: Ukiah Chamber of Commerce, 200 S. School St., Ukiah, CA 95482; (707) 462-4705 (WEB SITE: www.ukiahchamber.com; E-MAIL: info@ukiahchamber.com). Lake County Visitor Information Center, 875 Lakeport Blvd., Lakeport, CA 95453; (800) 525-3743 or (707) 263-5092 (WEB: www.lakecounty.com; E-MAIL info@lakecounty.com)

Northern Sonoma County

Although less known than Sonoma Valley to the south, this region is second only to the Napa Valley in total premium wine grapes, with more than 25,000 acres planted. A scenic southern extension of Mendocino County, northern Sonoma is a mix of tawny hills, redwood groves in hidden canyons and shady oak clusters bearded with Spanish moss. The region's gravelly, loamy soils along the flanks of the Russian River and Dry Creek produce some of America's premier wines. A few decades ago, this area was busy with hop yards and orchards. Some unused hop drying kilns survive, marked by their distinctive conical towers; a couple have been converted into wineries.

The first important vintners in this area were the brothers Korbel from Germany. Francis, Joseph and Anton settled along the Russian River in 1882, logged off the redwoods and began planting vineyards. The Korbel winery survives as the largest facility in the area. More European vintners followed and hundreds of acres soon were graced by vines. As in other areas, many of the wineries were closed by Prohibition. However, one optimistic Italian, John Pedroncelli, *started* a winery during this dry spell, figuring that it eventually would end. He was right of course and his sons John and Jim and their children run the operation today.

Our favorite vineland touring area, northern Sonoma County offers variety of uncrowded wineries, ranging from tiny and rustic to historically musty

> *Northern Sonoma offers a variety of uncrowded wineries.*

to grandiloquently modern. Several wineries are clustered around Healdsburg and a few tasting rooms, detached from their mother vineyards, are just off the charming town's plaza. Dry Creek Valley offers an excellent selection of wineries, as does the exceptionally scenic Westside Road leading into the Russian River Valley.

KINDS OF WINES: Generally warmer than southern Mendocino, this area yields excellent reds, particularly Zinfandel. It's also noted for fine Cabernet, Pinot Noir and Chardonnay. With a good selection of microclimates, it produces nearly all the popular varietals.

TO LEARN MORE: Free *Russian River Wine Road* maps covering most of northern Sonoma County are available from the Healdsburg Chamber of Commerce (address below) and the Sonoma County Wine and Visitors Center, 5000 Roberts Lake Rd., Rohnert Park, CA 94928; (707) 586-3795 (WEB SITE: sonomawine.com; E-MAIL: innfo@sonomawine.com).

Tourist information: Healdsburg Chamber of Commerce, 217 Healdsburg Ave., Healdsburg, CA 95448; (800) 648-9922; (707) 433-6935 (WEB: www.healdsburg.org; E-MAIL: hbgchamb@pacbell.net). Santa Rosa Chamber of Commerce, 637 First St., Santa Rosa, CA 95404, (707) 547-1414.

Sonoma Valley

This jewel of a basin, dubbed the "Valley of the Moon" by author Jack London, is rich in both vineyards and history. The last of California's missions was established here in 1823; it was the only one built under Mexican rule. In the 1830s when the Mexican government stripped the missions of their vast landholdings, young Mariano Guadalupe Vallejo was given the task of dissolving Mission San Francisco de Solano. He also laid out a town around a traditional Spanish plaza, calling it Sonoma, a name local Indians had given the valley.

As more Americans arrived in Alta California, Mexico began losing its grip on this northern outpost. On June 14, 1846, a rag-tag bunch of Sacramento Valley gringos marched on Sonoma, imprisoned an angry, sputtering Vallejo in his own barracks and proclaimed California to be an independent republic. It was the shortest republic on record. On July 9, a U.S. Naval force led by Commodore John Sloat captured Monterey to the south and annexed California to America.

An American supporter even before his imprisonment, Vallejo became the town's leading citizen and one of California's first major grape growers. Wayfaring Hungarian count Agoston Haraszthy arrived in 1856, bought some vineyard land from Vallejo and established Buena Vista Winery. It was to become the largest in California. As mentioned earlier, Haraszthy was sent abroad by Governor William Downey to collect premium grape cuttings and wine information from Europe. It's not an exaggeration to call him the father of California viticulture and Sonoma the cradle of the state's premium wine industry.

Another major Sonoma player was Samuele Sebastiani, who started a winery here in 1904. His son August became a legend in the industry. He was the first to introduce jug varietals and the first to bring the French *nouveau* tradition to America, releasing a Beaujolais within weeks of its bottling. Still family operated, Sebastiani Vineyards is the biggest facility in Sonoma and one of the world's largest privately owned wineries. Sam Sebastiani, Samuele's grandson, started his own operation, the Viansa Winery in the Carneros district between the Sonoma and Napa valleys.

The Sonoma Valley is a major visitor destination, second only to the Napa Valley among the state's vinelands. It's popular both as a wine producing area and as an important culinary center. Cheese, sausage and French bread producers on the plaza lure hungry visitors, and the town is noted for several fine restaurants. The mission and remnants of the Vallejo empire survive as elements of Sonoma State Historic Park. A ranch built by Jack London is in nearby Glen Ellen, part of another state park. Haraszthy's original Buena Vista Cellars was reopened several decades ago, and the venerable Sebastiani winery sits on the edge of town.

> *The Sonoma Valley is a major visitor destination, second only to the Napa Valley among the state's winelands.*

KINDS OF WINES: Blessed with a climatic mix, Sonoma Valley vintners offer a wide variety. Cabernet, Merlot and Zinfandel thrive here and the cool Carneros Region is suited to the sparkling wine classics of Chardonnay and Pinot Noir.

TO LEARN MORE: The *Sonoma Valley Visitors Guide* is available at many wineries and the Sonoma Valley Visitors Bureau (next page), or contact the Sonoma Valley Vintner's Association, 9 E. Napa St., Sonoma, CA 95476; (707) 935-0803 (WEB SITE: www.sonomavalleywine.com; E-MAIL: info@sonomavalleywine.com). Another good info source is the Sonoma County Wine and Visitors Center, 5000 Roberts Lake Rd., Rohnert Park, CA 94928, (707) 586-3795; (WEB: sonomawine.com; E-MAIL: innfo@sonomawine.com).

For tourist information: Sonoma Valley Visitors Bureau, 453 First St. East, Sonoma, CA 95476; (707) 996-1090 (WEB SITE: www.sonomavalley.com; E-MAIL: svvb@vom.com).

Napa Valley

Cradled between forest-clad hills, America's most famous wine valley presents an idyllic vision. Ranks of vines march along Highway 29 like an army in green camouflage. Ivy-walled wineries stand at roadside. Mansions built by yesterday's wine barons sulk behind protective cloaks of trees. The great bulk of Mount St. Helena commands the northern horizon.

The Napa Valley is everything you could hope for—and less. Nearly 250 wineries dot the basin; some of the larger ones draw 300,000 visitors a year. Tour buses may inundate tasting rooms without warning; insurance widows in blue rinse hairdos will giggle nervously and ask for a sip of something sweet. Highway 29 becomes traffic tangled on summer weekends.

Winery visits range from informal peeks into cellars to formal, educational tours.

Gimmicks such as the Napa Valley Wine Train, the "authentic" *City of Napa* sternwheeler and wine-theme shopping centers draw visitor hordes. Some wineries seem more concerned with selling T-shirts and picnic lunches than wines.

Yet, you can still find picturesque, tucked-away wineries with tasting rooms that are rarely crowded. You can discover winding country lanes bereft of cars, and lonely ramparts with valley vistas to draw your breath away. To avoid the mobs, visit the valley on an off-season weekday when even the larger wineries are uncrowded. Or focus on wineries away from Highway 29. Silverado Trail, just to the east and paralleling the highway, runs through more picturesque countryside in the Vaca foothills. Its wineries are much less crowded.

Many valley wineries charge for tasting, a practice which we do not find offensive. It discourages those out for a free drinking spree. Fees are quite nominal—three to five dollars to sample a variety of wines. Generally, you can keep the glass as a souvenir or apply the fee toward a bottle purchase.

Despite its touristy reputation, the valley is home to many serious vintners who produce some of America's finest wines. Not surprisingly, they're generally more expensive that similar varietals from other areas. Even unprocessed grapes command a higher price. They may be no better than comparable Sonoma fruit, but these are *Napa* grapes, thank you!

Although the valley has nearly 250 wineries, just ten of them control a third of the grape crop and produce forty percent of the wine. Among the larger ones are Charles Krug, Robert Mondavi, Beringer and Beaulieu—all household names. Historic Inglenook winery is now Neibaum-Coppola Estate, owned by a group that includes filmmaker Francis Ford Coppola.

Yet with all this viticultural largess, the Napa Valley produces only two percent of California's wine.

The first settler here was American frontiersman George Calvert Yount. After working for Sonoma's Vallejo, he was granted Rancho Caymus in the Napa Valley in the 1830s. He planted vineyards and orchards near the town named in his honor. John Patchett started the first commercial wine production in 1858. Then came families whose names still ring in Napa Valley history register: Charles Krug in 1860, Jacob Schram of Schramsberg in 1862, the Beringer brothers in the 1870s, Gustav Neibaum of Inglenook in 1899 and Georges de Latour, who established Beaulieu at the turn of the twentieth century.

Others left their marks on the valley as well. Flamboyant Mormon Sam Brannan, who shouted out the discovery of gold on the streets of San Francisco in 1848, built the valley's first mineral springs resort at Calistoga in 1868. During the summer of 1880, an impoverished, tubercular Scottish writer and his American bride spent their honeymoon in an old mining shack on the flanks of Mount St. Helena. From this visit came *The Silverado Squatters,* the first published writing of Robert Louis Stevenson.

Many of the valley's most prominent vintners arrived after the end of Prohibition. The Christian Brothers came in 1930 and built the impressive Greystone winery just outside St. Helena; it's now the Culinary Institute of America. Louis M. Martini established his operation in 1933 and Cesare Mondavi bought the Charles Krug winery ten years later. When Cesare died in 1959, it was passed to sons Robert and Peter. Robert left and in 1966 opened the valley's first new winery in twenty years. Indeed, the Robert Mondavi Winery was a new concept—designed not only for premium winemaking, but for public tours, vineyard concerts and other cultural events.

Despite its touristy reputation, the Napa Valley is home to many serious vintners who produce some of America's finest wines.

The valley offers lures beyond its vineyards, such as the undeveloped and scenic Robert Louis Stevenson State Park above Calistoga and glider rides in Calistoga, a couple of fine museums and more than a dozen hot air balloon companies. Curiously, the town of Napa—host to all this—is a rather ordinary middle-America community with almost none of the wine country's ambiance.

KINDS OF WINES: With a climate gradient tilting from the low Carneros plain to the flanks of Mount St. Helena, the valley is capable of producing virtually every major varietal. It is the American cradle of Cabernet Sauvignon; some wineries, such as Justin Meyer's Silver Oak, produce only that noble wine. Most vintners, however, offer a broad range. The Napa Valley and adjacent Carneros region are home to four major sparkling wine facilities: Domaine Carneros, Domaine Chandon, Mumm Napa Valley and Larkmead Vineyards. There's even a Japanese saké distillery and a brandy distillery in the valley's southern end.

TO LEARN MORE: The *Napa Valley Guide* with winery maps and listings of activities, restaurants and lodgings, is sold at wineries or it's available by mail from Vintage Publications, 2929 Conifer Ct., Napa, CA 94558 (WEB SITE: www.winecountry.com/guidebooks). The free *Silverado Trail* map produced by the Silverado Trail Wineries Association lists wineries on the "quiet side of the Napa Valley," available from member vintners, or call (800) 624-WINE.

For tourist information: Napa Chamber of Commerce, 1556 First St., Napa, CA 94559; (707) 226-7455 (WEB SITE: napachamber.org). Yountville Chamber of Commerce, P.O. Box 2064 (6516 Washington St.), Yountville, CA 94599; (707) 944-0904 (WEB SITE: www.yountville.com). St. Helena Chamber of Commerce, 1080 Main St., St. Helena, CA 94574; (800) 799-6456 or (707) 963-4456 (WEB SITE: www.sthelena.com). Calistoga Chamber of Commerce, 1458 Lincoln Ave., #9 (behind the Calistoga Depot), Calistoga, CA 94515; (707) 942-6333 (WEB SITE: www.calistogafun.com; E-MAIL: execdir@napanet.net).

The South Bay

Silicon chips and suburbs have prevailed over Sauvignon Blanc and Sémillon in southern Alameda and northern Santa Clara counties below San Francisco. However, many noteworthy wineries survive, even though most of their vines grow elsewhere. Only the Livermore Valley in the foothills south of Interstate 580 retains significant vineyard acreage.

These areas on the lower rim of San Francisco Bay appear on some of the earliest pages of California's wine history. Livermore Valley was settled by English sailor Robert Livermore, who picked up two Mexican land grants in 1830. He had wine grapes growing a decade later. Charles A. Wetmore, who served as California's chief viticultural officer, established Cresta Blanca Winery in 1882, followed by the arrival of Carl H. Wente and James Concannon the next year.

> **Early in the twentieth century, the Santa Clara Valley had more than 100 wineries and nearly 9,000 acres of vines.**

To the southwest, Santa Clara Valley's history reaches back even further. San José was born in 1777 as California's first civil settlement, when the area was still part of Spain. By the mid-1850s, it was a major wine producer and the surrounding Santa Clara Valley was called the "Garden Spot of the World."

French vineyardist Pierre Pellier started a winery here in 1854. His daughter married Pierre Mirassou in 1881, beginning the Mirassou wine dynasty that persists to this day. Early in the twentieth century, the Santa Clara Valley had more than 100 wineries and nearly 9,000 acres of vines. Today, it's mostly silicon chips, suburbs and service stations.

The few wineries here are usually uncrowded, although they're rather widespread and have to be sought out. The Wente and Mirassou facilities are quite pleasant, and the hilltop wineries of Santa Clara County's Montebello Ridge are fun to explore. The largest concentration of wineries—six of them—is south of Livermore.

KINDS OF WINES: Cooled by bay breezes, the Livermore and Santa Clara valleys are noted mostly for their whites, particularly Chardonnay, Sémillon, Sauvignon Blanc and Gray Riesling. Cabernet also does well here. The Montebello Ridge is noted for its Zinfandels.

TO LEARN MORE: The *Wines of Santa Clara Valley* map is available from wineries or the Santa Clara Valley Wine Growers Assn., P.O. Box 1192, Morgan Hill, CA 95037; (408) 778-1555 (WEB SITE: scvwga.com).

For tourist information: Livermore Chamber of Commerce, 2157 First St., Livermore, CA 94550; (925)

447-1606. San Jose Convention & Visitors Bureau, 333 W. San Carlos (in the San José Convention Center), San Jose, CA 95110; (800) SAN-JOSE or (408) 295-9600. (WEB: www.sanjose.org; E-MAIL: concierge@san-jose.org).

Southern Santa Clara Valley

This area ranks with northern Sonoma County as one of our favorite winery touring areas. The wines are excellent and affordable, the wineries are easy to find and the folks are friendly. The region's focal point is Gilroy, a town of 32,000 that's better known for garlic than for wine. Indeed, it produces a lot of both, al-though—like the San Jose area to the north—it's be-ginning to suffer suburban sprawl.

Locals don't mind being kidded about their garlicky reputation. In fact, they encourage it; highway signs proclaim Gilroy the Garlic Capital of the World. It's a rightful claim, since ninety percent of America's supply is produced hereabouts. To press this garlic issue, two stores on the south edge of town on Highway 101 and another downtown will sell you garlic-laced relish, mustard, marinade, jam, butter, ice cream and to clear your palate, garlic wine.

With all that garlic and all that wine, can Italians be far behind? The list of local vintners reads like a Milano phone book: Fortino, Conrotto, Rapazzini, Pedrizzetti and Guglielmo.

Neither garlic nor Italians figured into the area's early history. In the mid-nineteenth century, a dour Scotsman named John Cameron went AWOL from his British ship in Monterey Bay and scampered north-ward. Using his mother's maiden name of Gilroy to protect his identity, he married into the Ortega ranch-ing family, started a farm and became a pillar of the community.

This wasn't a major wine producing area until after the turn of the twentieth century. The largest winery in the region, Fortino, goes back only to 1970. A modern-day immigrant, Ernie Fortino came to America in 1959 and labored at other wineries until he saved enough money to start his own. His kids now run the operation and his brother Mario owns Hecker Pass winery next door.

This is an easy area to explore, since most of its wineries are concentrated along Highway 152 (Hecker Pass Highway) immediately west of Gilroy. A few others are north, near the town of Morgan Hill. Rapazzini, a winery and garlic shop, is just south of Gilroy on Highway 101. Wineries are uncrowded and all of them are small to medium-sized family operations.

KINDS OF WINES: These wooded, sunny hills are red wine country. Fine Zinfandel, Cabernet and Merlot wines emerge, along with less common varietals such as Grignolino, Carignan and Petite Sirah. A few whites are produced as well, notably Chardonnay, Johannisberg Riesling and Sauvignon Blanc.

TO LEARN MORE: A free *Wines of Santa Clara Valley* map is available at wineries or contact the Santa Clara Valley Wine Growers Association, P.O. Box 1192, Morgan Hill, CA 95037; (408) 779-2145 or (408) 778-1555.

For tourist information: Gilroy Visitors Bureau, 7780 Monterey Road, Gilroy, CA 95020; (408) 842-6436 (E-MAIL: visitorsbureau@gilroy.com).

Santa Cruz County

This county is a neat little package of mountains, redwood groves and an old fashioned seaside resort. Although it's noted mostly for beach frolic and hill country camping, it does offer a few wineries, all small and mostly family-owned.

The county's largest community traces its roots from Mission Santa Cruz (sainted cross), established in 1791. The surrounding mountains were logged heavily for their redwoods when the Americans came, although some fine groves have been preserved in several state parks. The Bargetto Winery in Soquel just east of Santa Cruz dates from 1933, although the rest are of quite recent vintage. Most are tucked into the thickets of the Santa Cruz Mountains.

Like the Gilroy area, most Santa Cruz wineries are family owned, so your visit will be rather personal. Other than Bargetto, they're quite small. Workers at Gallo probably spill more wine than these small vintners produce. The wineries are rather widespread, and it takes a bit of mountain driving to ferret out most of them, although they're worth the effort of discovery.

KINDS OF WINES: The county's sun-warmed hills produce rather good Chardonnay, Cabernet and Pinot Noir; most of the other major whites and reds are bottled here as well. Bargetto specializes in fruit wines, in addition to a variety of wines from the grape.

TO LEARN MORE: *Fine Wines of Santa Cruz* brochures are available at wineries, or contact the Santa Cruz Mountains Winegrowers Association, 7605-A Old Dominion Ct., Aptos, CA 95003; (831) 479-9463 (WEB SITE: www.webwinery.com/scmwa).

For tourist information: Santa Cruz Conference and Visitors Council, 701 Front St., Santa Cruz, CA 95060; (800) 833-3494 or (831) 425-1234 (WEB SITE: santacruzca.org; E-MAIL: info@scccrc.org).

Monterey County

Noted primarily for tourism, Steinbeck novels and golf tournaments, Monterey County offers a vineyard surprise. It contains nearly 30,000 acres of premium wine grapes—more than any other California county except Napa and Sonoma. They're not that evident, however. There is no great gathering of wineries, and the only concentration of tasting rooms is in that mother of all tourist traps, Monterey's Cannery Row.

Many wineries offer picnic areas among their vines.

Most of the vines are in the cool, flat and wind-brushed Salinas Valley below Salinas, although you won't see many from the main highway, U.S. 101. They're coved into the Gavilan Mountain benchlands to the east and the Santa Lucias to the west.

Although Monterey County is certainly rich in the lore of early California, it wasn't a serious wine-producing area until the 1970s. It was thought to be too dry and windy. Then, aided by researchers from the University of California at Davis, growers solved the wind problem by planting grapes parallel to prevailing breezes. Drilling proved that the Salinas River, running mostly underground, had plenty of water for irrigation.

Three area wineries are easily reached, just off Highway 101 between Gonzales and Greenfield. Four tasting rooms are divorced from the vineyards, conveniently grouped on Cannery Row. One—Paul Masson—includes a rather attractive wine museum. Of course, the Monterey-Carmel area is a major tourist destination with lots of historic sites, the excellent Monterey Bay Aquarium and scenic oceanfront.

KINDS OF WINES: Since it's a cool, breezy area, the county's flatlands are ideal for whites, which account for seventy-five percent of the vines. Among those that thrive are Chardonnay (the most commonly planted variety), Sauvignon Blanc and Gewürztraminer. Cabernet Sauvignon is the most popular red; Zinfandel, Pinot Noir, Petite Sirah and Merlot are among its ruby companions.

TO LEARN MORE: A *Monterey Wine Country* "passport" directs sippers to various wineries. It's available at visitor centers or from Monterey Wine Country Associates; (831) 375-9400.

For tourist information: Monterey Peninsula Visitors & Convention Bureau, P.O. Box 1770, Monterey, CA 93942; (831) 649-1770 (WEB SITE: www.monterey.com; E-MAIL: ucb@redshift.com).

South Central Coast

This area shelters the California wine country's biggest surprise. It's alive with interesting wineries, from family funky to corporately elegant. Shared by Santa Barbara and San Luis Obispo counties, it's the state's fastest-growing wine district. Some of the wineries rival the most opulent Napa and Sonoma facilities. Further, many are in rather appealing, bucolic river valleys that are flanked by thickly wooded hills.

Vines and wineries are focused in four areas, two in each of the counties. Santa Barbara's vinelands are in the Santa Ynez Valley around Solvang and Buellton, and in the Santa Maria Valley, east of the town by that name. San Luis Obispo's vineyards are concentrated in the Edna Valley inland from Arroyo Grande, and around Paso Robles to the north. Compared to Napa and Sonoma, this region be-

> *Compared to Napa and Sonoma, this region became a major wine producer almost overnight.*

came a major wine producer almost overnight. All but two of the wineries have emerged since the 1970s.

Since this area is still being discovered, the wineries are relatively uncrowded. The region contains other lures as well, such as the Danish village of Solvang, the resort city of Santa Barbara to the south, and the nearby beaches of Pismo and Avila. San Luis Obispo is an attractive mission and university town.

KINDS OF WINES: Cool breezes and morning fogs temper the summer sun, creating the proper climate for Chardonnay and other mild-weather whites, plus Merlot, Cabernet Sauvignon and Pinot Noir. The warmer Paso Robles area produces fine Zinfandels.

TO LEARN MORE: Three free touring maps are available: *Wineries of the Edna Valley and Arroyo Grande,* from Edna Valley Arroyo Grande Vintners, P.O. Box 159, Arroyo Grande, CA 93420; (805) 541-5868. *Wine Tasting in Paso Robles*, from Paso Robles Vintners and Growers, P.O. Box 324 (1940 Sprint St.), Paso Robles, CA 93446 (WEB SITE: www.pasowine.com; E-MAIL: prvga@pasowine.com). *Santa Barbara County Wineries,* available from the Santa Barbara County Vintners' Association, P.O. Box 1558, Santa Ynez, CA 93460-1558; (805) 688-0881 (WEB SITE: www.sbcountywines.com; E-MAIL: info@sbcounty-wines.com).

For tourist information: San Luis Obispo Chamber of Commerce, 1039 Chorro St., San Luis Obispo, CA

93446; (805) 781-2777 (WEB SITE: visitslo.com; E-MAIL: slochamber@slochamber.org). Solvang Conference & Visitors Bureau, P.O. Box 70, Solvang, CA 93464; (800) 468-6765 or (805) 688-6144 (WEB SITE: www.solvangusa.com; E-MAIL: scvb@svv.com). Paso Robles Chamber of Commerce, 1113 Spring St., Paso Robles, CA 93446; (805) 238-0506.

The Gold Country

No single region looms larger in California's history than the Sierra Nevada foothills. Here, the discovery of gold in 1848 catapulted a remote Mexican outpost into the most populous and prosperous state in the Union. This also was one of the state's first wine producing areas, with a hundred wineries operating in the late 1800s. However, dwindling population as the gold ran out, followed by phylloxera and Prohibition, virtually eliminated the industry. Only one, D'Agostini Winery, traces its roots back to the Gold Rush. It was purchased in 1989 by the Sobon family and re-christened Sobon Estate; it's now primarily a wine museum.

The current winery boom started in the 1970s, with the discovery by U.C. Davis scientists that these well-drained slopes were ideal for Zinfandel and several other varietals. Hot summer afternoons, cool alpine nights and tough granite soil produce high-sugar, high-acid grapes that ripen late, sometime between deer season and the first rains.

Wineries are grouped in four areas: El Dorado County, northeast of Placerville off Highway 50; south of there, off Mount Aukum Road; in Amador County's Shenandoah Valley east of Plymouth, probably the best Zinfandel country in the state; and near the charming old mining town of Murphys in Calaveras County.

Gold country wineries are inviting places, often in attractive wooded settings or pretty foothill valleys. Most are small and family-owned. Also, a trip to the gold country is a journey into California history, for the area abounds with old mining towns, museums, historic parks and Gold Rush hotels. Popular ski areas are just above, and several reservoirs in the foothills offer water sports.

Murphys is a particularly inviting wine touring area, since wineries are closely grouped, and three tasting rooms are right in town. Columbia State Historic Park, the most visited attraction in the gold country, is just across New Melones Reservoir in neighboring Tuolumne County.

KINDS OF WINES: This is where you go for a little Zin, or a lot if you have an appetite like ours. Zinfandel and other reds—Cabernet, Merlot and Pinot Noir—are typically robust, spicy and full-flavored. El Dorado County, whose vineyards are mostly at higher elevations, produces fine whites, primarily Chardonnay and Sauvignon Blanc.

TO LEARN MORE: These winery map-guides will steer you through the gold country's wine country: *El Dorado Wine Country,* El Dorado Vintners Association, P.O. Box 1614, Placerville, CA 95667; (800) 306-3956 or (530) 446-6562 (WEB SITE: www.eldoradowines.org). *Amador County Wine Country*, Amador Vintners Association, c/o the Amador County Chamber of Commerce (see below). *Calaveras, the Other Wine Country*, Calaveras Wine Association, P.O. Box 2492, Murphys, CA 95247; (800) 225-3764 (WEB SITE: www.calaveraswines.org; E-MAIL: info@calaveraswines.org).

For tourist information: Amador County Chamber of Commerce, P.O. Box 596, Jackson, CA 95642; (800) 649-4988 or (209) 223-0350 (WEB SITE: www.amadorcountychamber.net). Calaveras Visitors Bureau, P.O. Box 367, Angels Camp, CA 95222; (800) 225-3764 or (209) 736-0049 (WEB SITE: www.visitcalaveras.org; EMAIL: frogmail@calaveras.org). El Dorado County Chamber of Commerce, 542 Main St., Placerville, CA 95667; (800) 457-6279 or (530) 621-5885 9 (WEB SITE: www.eldoradocounty.org; E-MAIL: chamber@eldoradocounty.org).

Temecula Valley

In the beginning, California's population was centered in the northern end of the state and wine production was focused in the south. Now, of course, the roles are reversed.

Pioneer planters such as Jean Louis Vignes and William Wolfskill made Los Angeles the "city of vineyards" in the 1830s. A utopian colony of Germans planted thousands of vines in Anaheim, not far from a land now ruled by Mickey Mouse. Urban sprawl has inundated all of the Southland's original vineyard areas; only a few isolated wineries survive. The last wine producing region to go under asphalt was the Cucamonga district near Riverside and San Bernardino, where the final wineries closed in the 1960s.

A decade later, a new home was found for southern California's wine country—the Temecula Valley between Riverside and San Diego. It's in southern Riverside County, about fifteen miles from the Pacific Ocean, close enough to benefit from ocean breezes. Although it's the state's southernmost wine producing area, it's rather cool. Those breezes and a 1,300-foot elevation provide proper climate for whites.

This area hasn't escaped the unending Southland population sprawl. Since the first vines were planted in the 1970s, Temecula has rocketed from a quiet, wanna-be-cowboy hamlet into a community of more than 30,000. However, the vineyards are in a protected agricultural zone, east of the mushrooming city. Here, they share dry, sandy hillocks with avocado groves, fancy horse ranches and a remarkable tally of luxurious country estates. This is one of America's newest vineyard areas. Of a dozen wineries in the valley, only one—Callaway—existed in 1974.

Although somewhat scattered over the sandy hills, the wineries are relatively easy to find. The local chamber of commerce's visitor guide has a map in its centerfold. The area offers a good mix of wineries, from small family affairs to some rather elaborate corporate-owned facilities. Although the Temecula Valley is far removed from most of the rest of California's vineyard area, it's certainly easy to reach if you're in southern California.

KINDS OF WINES: Chardonnay and Sauvignon Blanc are the most popular varietals, and they're often excellent. We've also tasted some highly drinkable Cabernet, Merlot and Petite Sirah.

TO LEARN MORE: The *Temecula Valley Visitors Guide* contains a map and details of area wineries. It's available from vintners or from the Temecula Valley Chamber of Commerce, 27450 Santa Ynez Rd., Suite 104, Temecula, CA 92591; (909) 676-5090.

Oregon Wine Regions

OREGON

Oregonians have never liked Californians much. Outnumbered more than ten to one, they constantly suffer the trespass of their neighbors from the south, who crowd their towns and highways, buy up the land and bring their "California ways" to this rather provincial state.

However, few of them begrudge the many California winemakers who have come north, planted vines and produced wines that rival and even excel those of the Golden State.

The state's wine industry started in the 1850s when pioneer photographer and horticulturist Peter Britt planted vines near the gold rush town of Jacksonville in southwestern Oregon. However, Prohibition closed all of the early wineries. The oldest contemporary vineyards date from the 1960s. And most of those were started by Californians.

Richard Sommer, a viticultural graduate from U.C. Davis, headed for the Umpqua Valley near Roseburg in 1961. He was convinced that this climate and terrain—similar to that of Germany—would produce good Rieslings; his Hillcrest Winery is still proving his point. A second U.C. Davis grad, David Lett, pressed even farther north and planted Pinot Noir grapes near McMinnville in the upper Willamette Valley. His Eyrie Winery soon began winning serious awards in California and France, particularly for its Pinot Noir.

Oregon ranks fourth behind California, New York and Washington in American wine production, and second in the number of wineries. More than 130 wineries—nearly twice as many as a decade ago—are concentrated in a thin north-south strip between the Coast and Cascade mountain ranges. This is an area of cool, soggy winters and warm, often overcast summer days. The topography, climate and latitude are similar to that of many French and German wine areas.

The Willamette Valley between Portland and Eugene is the state's largest wine producing area. Another dozen wineries are in Washington County west of Portland and half a dozen are in the Umpqua Valley. A few more are scattered about southwestern Oregon in the Bear Creek and Rogue River valleys and Illinois Valley.

Oregon's wine industry takes itself very seriously, imposing the nation's strictest labeling laws. You'll find no burgundies, chablis or champagnes here, since laws forbid their use as generic names. Varietal wines must contain ninety percent of the named grape (seventy-five percent for Cabernet Sauvignon) and vintage labeled wines must contain ninety-five percent of grapes from the stated year. An appellation can't be used unless all wine in the bottle came from that area.

Most Oregon wineries are small and family-owned, often sharing pretty rolling hill countryside with orchards, pasturelands, forests and berry vines. (The state is famous for its berry wines.)

TO LEARN MORE: For a free copy of the brochure *Discover Oregon Wineries,* contact the Oregon Winegrowers Association, 1200 NW Naito Parkway, Suite 400, Portland, OR 97209; (800) 242-2363. Another useful source is the monthly *Oregon Wine Magazine,* available at most wineries. To order the most recent copy by mail, call (503) 232-7607.

Willamette Valley

Yamhill County is Oregon's largest wine producing area, with a fourth of the state's vineyards and about thirty wineries with tasting rooms open to the public. Another fair gathering of vineyards and wineries is south between Salem and Eugene. Highway 99W is the main corridor through both areas. The Yambill County landscape around McMinnville, Lafayette, Dundee and Newberg is as pleasing a bucolic image as you'll find anywhere in America. Hundreds of acres of vines dance over gently rolling hills like green hooked rugs.

KINDS OF WINES: This is Pinot Noir country, producing some of the best versions of this classic varietal on the planet. Most winemakers offer other varieties as well, particularly Riesling, Pinot Gris, Chardonnay and Pinot Blanc. Some growers are now using Chardonnay clones from France.

TO LEARN MORE: For maps of Willamette Valley wineries, contact the Yamhill County Wineries Association, P.O. Box 25162, Portland OR 97298, (503) 646-2985 (WEB SITE://oregonwine.org/wine/yamhill; E-MAIL: yamwine@teleport.com); and South Willamette Wine Growers, P.O. Box 1591, Eugene, OR 97440. Tourist information is available from the Greater McMinnville Chamber of Commerce, 417 NW Adams St., McMinnville, OR 97128, (503) 472-6196; and the Newberg Chamber of Commerce, 115 N. Washington St., Newberg, OR 97132, (503) 538-2014. (WEB: newberg.org; E-MAIL: nacc@teleport.com)

Washington County

Tucked between the Cascades and the Coast Range, Washington County's Tualatin Valley west of Portland is a pretty region of farmlands, dairies, tree-thatched rolling hills and about a dozen wineries.

KINDS OF WINES: This cool, damp climate produces Pinot Noir, Pinot Gris, Chardonnay, Müller-Thurgau, Gewürztraminer, Riesling and—at one small operation—Japanese saké.

TO LEARN MORE: For a *Wineries of Washington County* touring guide, contact: Convention & Visitors Bureau of Washington County, P.O. Box 803, Beaverton, OR 97075-0803; (800) 537-3149 or (503) 644-5555. (WEB SITE: www.wcva.org)

Umpqua Valley

Head briefly southwest from the old, well-kept lumering town of Roseburg and you'll encounter half a dozen small ineries. While not as pretty as the Yamhill vinelands, the Umpqua Valley presents a pleasant picture of low, wooded hills, pasturelands and orchards. Blue and white directional signs steer winetasters on a forty-two mile course through this rural landscape.

KINDS OF WINES: This is one of the few areas in the American northwest warm enough to produce Zinfandel, that sun-loving grape so popular in California. Cabernet Sauvignon and Pinot Noir also do well here, along with whites such as Chardonnay, Riesling and Gewürztraminer.

TO LEARN MORE: For a winery map and tourist information, contact the Roseburg Visitors & Convention Bureau, P.O. Box 1262 (410 SE Spruce St.), Roseburg, OR 97470; (800) 444-9584 or (541) 672-9731 (WEB SITE: www.visitroseburg.com; E-MAIL: info@visitroseburg.com).

Southwestern Oregon

The scenic Rogue River Valley is one of Oregon's most popular tourist areas. Hundreds of thousands, mostly Californians, come for its whitewater rafting, plus nearby Crater Lake National Park, Oregon Caves National Monument, Oregon Shakespeare Festival in Ashland and Jacksonville's Britt music festivals. Southwestern Oregon also has a sprinkling of wineries. A few are near Ashland and Jacksonville in the Bear Creek/Rogue River valleys, and two more are in the Illinois Valley on the way to the Oregon Caves.

KINDS OF WINES: With hotter and drier summers than Oregon's other viticultural areas, southwestern wineries produce very good Merlot and Pinot Noir, plus whites such as Chardonnay and Gewürztraminer.

FOR MORE INFORMATION: These tourist offices can provide material on nearby wineries. Ashland Chamber of Commerce, P.O. Box 1360 (110 E. Main St.), Ashland, OR 97520; (541) 482-3486 (WEB SITE: www.ashlandchamber.com; E-MAIL: chamber2cmind.net). Grants Pass Visitors & Convention Bureau, 1995 NW Vine St., Grants Pass, OR 97526; (800) 547-5927 or (541) 476-5510 (WEB: www.visitgrantspass.org). Jacksonville Chamber of Commerce, P.O. Box 33 (185 N. Oregon St.), Jacksonville, OR 97530; (541) 899-8118.

Washington
Wine
Regions

WASHINGTON

Leon Adams, the highly respected California wine writer, once called the award-winning Washington state wine industry "a miracle."

What seems miraculous is that any kind of vine would grow in the state's main wine producing region, let alone superior varietals. The eastern two-thirds of the state is a vast desert and prairie, cut by deep, narrow ravines of the Columbia and Snake rivers. They were gouged through layers of basalt by "Missoula Floods" when ice dams shattered and great walls of water surged downstream 15,000 years ago. The rain-shadow thrown by the Cascade Range makes this an arid land, although the two large rivers provide an abundance of water for irrigation. Indeed, eastern Washington is one of the largest agricultural areas outside of California's Central Valley.

But, could this desert-prairie grow wine grapes? In 1902, William Bridgman from Canada proved that it could; he planted Cabernet Sauvignon and Riesling vines near the town with the funny double-jointed name, Walla Walla. The climate was ideal in this high prairie, with warm summer days, cool nights and a long frost-free growing season. Never mind that it bears no resemblance to the Rhine, Bordeaux or Napa Valley. As long as water was available, it could grow excellent grapes, high in both sugar and acid. However, Prohibition closed down the early efforts, then Washington laws, which controlled the sale of alcohol, inhibited further winery growth.

Several amateur winemakers led by Lloyd Woodburne, a psychology professor at Seattle University, started producing wines in his garage (not his bathtub) in the 1950s, using grapes from the Yakima Valley. In 1962, so they could legally sell their wine, they incorporated as Associated Vintners. Noted wine writer Adams and legendary winemaker André Tchelistcheff praised some of their wines and the company prospered. Associated Vintners eventually became Columbia Winery, one of the state's largest. Other wineries followed—large and small—and today Washington is America's third largest wine producer, and the second largest maker of premium wines, after California.

Three areas—the Walla Walla, Yakima and Columbia valleys—have been designated Approved Viticultural Areas (AVA) and they produce most of the state's wines. Several other wineries are along the Columbia and Snake rivers northwest of Spokane in northeastern Washington. A few more are in the Puget Sound area although they've not met with the success of the inland wineries. Incidentally, Washington wine grape production started in the Puget Sound region, stretching back to the 1870s on Stretch Island.

TO LEARN MORE: For a free touring guide to the Evergreen State's wineries, contact the Washington Wine Commission, 500 Union, Seattle, WA 98101; (206) 667-9463 (WEB SITE: www.washingtonwine.org; E-MAIL: jdoak@washingtonwine.org).

Walla Walla Valley

Although this area of southeastern Washington near the Oregon border was one of the state's first viticultural regions, wineries are few and rather scattered. Its central city is Walla Walla with a population around 26,000. Most of the wineries are just to the west in a farm belt that's also busy with row crops, wheat fields, dairy farms and onion patches. The "Walla Walla sweet" is regarded as the best onion this side of Maui.

KINDS OF WINES: Merlot, Cabernet Sauvignon and Chardonnay do particularly well in this area, which is the coolest of the state's eastern Cascade vineyard areas. Some wineries also produce tasty Rieslings.

TO LEARN MORE: For details on wineries and other tourist lures, contact the Walla Walla area Chamber of

Commerce at P.O. Box 644 (29 E. Sumach St.), Walla Walla, WA 99362; (877) WW-VISIT or (509) 525-0850 (WEB SITE: www.wwchamber.com; E-MAIL: info@wwchamber.com).

Yakima Valley

When folks want to go Washington winery touring, this is generally where they go. Southeast of the city of Yakima, this slender valley has the largest collection of wineries in the state. Unlike the Walla Walla and Columbia Valley districts that border the Columbia River, the Yakima Valley is about fifty miles north of that great stream. Incidentally, this is no Napa Valley; vineyards share gentle, unforested hills with fruit orchards, row crops and hops. The Yakima region is considered the fruit capital of the American Northwest.

Serious wine country begins about twenty miles southeast of Yakima, just beyond two towns with funny names—Toppenish and Zillah. Wineries stretch for fifty-five miles eastward, between here and Benton City. However, the largest concentration—in fact the *only* concentration—is around Zillah, a cute and well-maintained old farm town. The area's largest winery, Chateau Ste. Michelle, is in an industrial area in the town of Grandview. As we said, this isn't the Napa Valley.

KINDS OF WINES: Chateau Ste. Michelle offers a full roster of wines while other area wineries—mostly small and family-owned—are more focused. Among varietals that thrive here are Riesling, Sémillon, Cabernet Sauvignon, Merlot, Chardonnay and Sauvignon Blanc.

TO LEARN MORE: *Yakima Valley Wine Tour* and *Fruit Loop* guide maps are available from the Toppenish Chamber of Commerce, P.O. Box 28, Toppenish, WA 98948; (800) 569-3982 or (509) 865-3262 (WEB SITE: www.toppenish.org; E-MAIL: chamber@toppenish.org). Zillah Chamber of Commerce, P.O. Box 1294 (503 N. First Ave.), Zillah, WA 98953; (509) 829-5055.

Columbia Valley

Although Columbia Valley is a Designated Viticultural Area, the valley itself also encompasses the Walla Walla and Yakima valleys. The specific AVA applies to patches of land along the Columbia River on the Oregon border, plus segments to the north, above the confluence of the Columbia and Snake. Its climate and wines are similar to those of the Yakima Valley. There are no concentrations of wineries in this rather scattered district. However, some of the state's largest are here, including Columbia Crest, occupying a spectacular setting above the river.

NEW YORK STATE

You've no doubt heard of the old movie title, *A Tree Grows in Brooklyn*. But, grapevines? New York is the second largest wine producing state after California and its first vines were planted not in upstate rural areas, but on Long Island and in Brooklyn. In fact, a winery functioned in Brooklyn right up to Prohibition.

Since this was one of the first areas of America to be settled, it also was among the first to begin wine production. In the 1640s, nearly a century and a half before Spanish padres cultivated vines in California, vineyards were planted on Long Island. Attempts at growing classic European *vinifera* failed because sub-zero winter temperatures killed the dormant vines, so early winemakers had to settle for the native *labrusca*. Varieties called Isabella and Catawba proved to be successful in the chilly climate.

By the late 1600s, winemaking had spread to upstate New York, particularly to the Hudson River Valley to the north, where French settlers started vineyards in 1677. This is the oldest still-active wine producing region in America. New York vintners did so well that they soon were producing enough wine to serve all of Britain's American colonies. Vintners gradually worked eastward and by the 1800s, vines were flourishing on the shores of Lake Erie south of Buffalo and in the scenic Finger Lakes District, an area of slender glacial-carved ponds below Lake Ontario. Meanwhile, because of problems with mildew and fungus, wine production virtually ceased in the area where it had begun—on Long Island.

Because most New York state vineyards were planted with phylloxera-resistant native grapes, wine-makers were spared that scourge in the late 1800s. However, they were not spared the prohibitionist movement; in fact, it had its roots among New York's

New York
Wine
Regions

Buffalo

Chautauqua
Lake Erie
Niagara

Finger
Lakes
Region

The Finger
Lakes

Hudson River

Hudson
Valley

Long Island
New York

vineyards. In the 1870s, nearly half a century before Prohibition began, the Women's Christian Temperance Union created such a fuss that some growers started switching to grapes more suitable to eating than fermenting. Two dentist brothers named Welsh, who favored prohibition, began producing and selling grape juice late in the century, and their popular product survives to this day.

When Prohibition with a capital "P" began in 1919, New York grape growers were better positioned for survival than those in California. Their Concord and other American varieties were more suited to grape juice and sacramental wines, which were permitted. Grape bricks which could be dissolved in water, and juices with names like Virginia Dare Tonic were popular. Yeast already was present in these products and warning labels advised people not to keep them too long or they would ferment.

After Repeal, California quickly surged ahead of New York in premium wine production. Some of its classic grape vineyards had survived Prohibition and others were quickly replanted.

"As the Californians moved toward Cabernet Sauvignon, the New Yorkers were stuck with Concord and Catawba," wrote Robert Joseph in *The Wines of the Americas* (Salamander Books, London, © 1990).

Although the New York wine industry continued to grow during the middle years of the twentieth century, it still relied primarily on American *labrusca* and weather-hardy hybrid varieties. The breakthrough came in the 1950s when Russian immigrant Konstanin Frank insisted that classic French vines grafted onto the right rootstock could survive the state's subzero winters. He began working with vintner Charles Fournier, a successful sparkling wine maker. Eventually, they settled on rootstock from Quebec, Canada. In the winter of 1957, when 25-below-zero weather damaged native American vines, their grafted Chardonnay and Riesling survived.

Today, some of America's largest winemakers thrive in New York state, including Taylor, now owned by Seagram, and Canandaigua, which has expanded westward and operates wineries in California.

TO LEARN MORE: Contact the New York Wine and Grape Foundation, 350 Elm St., Penn Yan, NY 14527; (315) 536-7442 (WEB SITE: www.nywine.com).

Long Island

Although winemakers had given up on Long Island more than a century earlier because of the wet climate, this has become the state's newest wine country. Using modern sprays that kill damp weather fungus, winemakers began planting French varietals in the 1970s. They are producing some of the state's best wines in the islands's warm microclimates. Land is very expensive on this slender island that's a popular weekend retreat for wealthy New Yorkers, although a dozen or more wineries are thriving.

KINDS OF WINES: With a climate similar to that of Bordeaux, Long Island produces fine Cabernet Sauvignon, Chardonnay, Merlot, Pinot Noir and Riesling. Virtually all vineyards here are planted in European varietals and it's considered one of the best premium wine areas east of California.

Hudson Valley & Chautauqua-Niagara

Although the Hudson River Valley was one of the first important wine producing areas outside the New York City area, vineyards have diminished to fewer than a thousand acres. Because of its cold winters, virtually all vines are native American, cold-weather hybrids or European grafts. The small Chautauqua-Niagara region on the shores of Lake Erie has a longer growing season than the Hudson Valley, but the winters are frigid. (Ask anyone who's attended a late-season Buffalo Bills' game.) It produces mostly grape juice and kosher wines, although a few grafted premium varietals have been planted.

KINDS OF WINES: To withstand the winter chill, hybrids are used to make jug whites and light red wines in the Hudson River Valley, although grafted premium vines are producing Chardonnay, Riesling, Cabernet Sauvignon, Merlot and Gewürztraminer. Chautauqua-Niagara makes mostly kosher and dessert wines from Concord grapes.

Finger Lakes

This pretty area laced with glacial carved lakes is *the* New York state winemaking area, home to multi-million-gallon producers such as Taylor and Canandaigua. It's the largest American vineyard area outside California, with more than 15,000 acres planted. In fact, more than half the American wine produced outside the Golden State comes from Finger Lakes.

Because of its climate extremes, this area continues to grow mostly native American *labrusca* vines along with some weather-resistant hybrids. Canandaigua still bottles that Prohibition-defying "Virginia Dare," which is the oldest wine label in America. A few *vinifera* vineyards survive in some microclimate enclaves that are spared the region's savage winters.

KINDS OF WINES: Simple table wines and inexpensive sparkling wines fill most of the vats and bottles in the Finger Lakes district. Areas blessed with more suitable microclimates produce good Chardonnay, Pinot Noir, Cabernet Sauvignon and sweet late harvest Riesling.

Chapter four

APPRECIATING
WINE
What if I don't like it?

Roman author and philosopher Pliny wrote about the merits of wine around the time of Christ, as we noted in the opening chapter. He put down French wines as inferior to those of Rome, thus becoming history's first wine snob. He did not, however, say:

It's a naive, domestic Burgundy without much breeding, but I think you'll be amused by its presumption.

That was a cartoon caption by James Thurber in the *New Yorker*.

We now present, in simplified form, our three basic steps to wine enjoyment without snobbery. Follow this advice and you will be at ease in the sometimes confusing world of wine appreciation:

1. KNOW YOUR SUBJECT: This isn't as difficult as it sounds. On the pages that follow, you will learn everything you need to know to become a wine aficionado. Not a wine connoisseur, but an aficionado. The difference? An aficionado is one who knows enough about the wine in his or her glass to savor and appreciate it. A connoisseur knows which corner of the vineyard the grapes came from and whether the crusher removed his socks first.

2. DRINK THE WINE YOU ENJOY: Don't be intimidated by wine *chic* or fads. Never mind if your wine smug friends insist that a French Bordeaux whose name you can't pronounce is the required accompaniment to steak Diane. If you're a beginning wine enthusiast, you may find dry reds a bit too tart. Most wine neophytes are more comfortable with whites, perhaps with a tiny hint of residual sugar. (It's not cool to refer to a white table wine as sweet; just say it's slightly off-dry.)

3. MOVE ON TO MORE INTERESTING WINES: Learn to appreciate drier wines with their more subtle flavors, bouquets and aromas. Although off-dry wines may be more palatable initially, that touch of sugar masks its many flavor nuances and aromatic subtleties. Most wine novices advance from the bunny slope to the intermediate runs, drinking progressively drier types. With time and patience, they can progress to the black diamond runs of aged Cabernet Sauvignon or a rare full-bodied Zinfandel.

But, you ask (blinking innocently), why should I force myself to drink something that doesn't taste good?

When my son Dan was about seven, we decided that we were both mature enough to go on the Space Mountain ride at Disneyland. He stood stoically in line, wincing as he heard the screams coming from within the dark void before us.

After we were in the car, climbing inexorably to the top of the first drop—when it was too late to back out—he asked in that wonderfully timid little child's voice:

"What if I don't like it?"

"Then you won't have to do it again," I said quietly. "But you know it won't hurt you, because all these other people are doing it. And you'll never know if you like something unless you—ahhhhhhh!"

Our car plummeted downward through the blackness and I yelled louder than he did.

If we didn't teach ourselves to like things that were strange and perhaps intimidating, we'd lead pretty dull lives. We'd still be eating white bread and drinking tap water. Part of the adventure in life is educating ourselves to new tastes and sensations.

In the end, if you just can't get your palate trained to a Silver Oaks Cabernet Sauvignon, you can always retreat to an off-dry Chenin Blanc.

To appreciate wine, you must first learn how to taste it. All that sloshing and sniffing practiced by winetasters isn't supercilious nonsense. Many subtleties lurk in a bottle of wine, as we've already noted. Only by following a few basic steps can you discern all the nuances of the essence of the grape.

A favorite little story among aficionados concerns French statesman Charles Maurice de Tallyrand, who was teaching a young charge how to properly appreciate wine.

"First, you must hold your glass to the light and swirl the wine slowly to study its color. Then, bring it to your nose and breathe the wine's bouquet."

"And then?" the neophyte asked eagerly.

"And then, young man, you set your glass down and you talk about it."

However, as Carlo Rossi used to say in those old TV commercials, we'd rather drink our wine than talk about it.

To begin the tasting ritual, put about an ounce of wine into a glass. That's the typical pour at a winery tasting room, providing enough of a sample to sniff and sip, while leaving plenty of room to swirl it around. (A few wineries, unfortunately, serve their samples in silly little plastic cups, more suited to holding catsup for your fries.)

The receptacle should be a clear, stemmed wine glass with more or less of a tulip shape. The inward curving of the glass acts as a chimney, directing the aroma and bouquet to your nose for the sniffing part of the ritual. (We'll have more on glassware later in this chapter.)

Your wine sample should be neither too cold nor too warm, since either extreme will mask the subtle smell and taste. This is true both for sampling and regular drinking. Whites should be sipped at about fifty to fifty-five degrees, reds about sixty to sixty-five. We're not sure who started this rumor about serving red wines at "room temperature." The typical room is heated to seventy-two degrees, and you don't really want to drink your wine lukewarm. Cellar temperature is a better description, referring to the temperature at which reds are stored.

And now, on to the ritual:

SEE • Take the glass by the stem, hold it up to the light and examine the wine for clarity. It should be—pardon the old Nixon cliché—perfectly clear, with no

cloudy or murky appearance. A wine with absolute clarity is described as "brilliant." White wines are never white; they range from nearly colorless to deep straw to burnished gold. Some have hints of green; a Gewürztraminer may show a touch of pink, betraying its creation from a rosy-skinned grape. Often, you can tell a wine's age by its color—particularly a red. A youth can range from vermilion to deep purple. As it ages, it may show shades of caramel, particularly around its thin edges if you tilt the glass. The French, who get terribly poetic about these things, call a wine's color its "gown."

Don't panic if you detect minute particles in a glass of wine. They may be harmless bits of cork or, in the case of aged reds, tannin residue or tartrate crystals that were stirred up when the wine was poured. They should not affect the taste of the wine.

SLOSH • Coat the inside of the glass by swirling the wine around vigorously (being careful, of course, that you don't slosh it all over the individual next to you.) A good way to stabilize your glass is to keep the base on a counter or table, grasp it by the stem or base, and scoot it around in a rapid circular motion.

SNIFF • Hold the glass up to your nose—the closer the better; get that beak in there—and inhale deeply. The sloshing and coating action will have released all the wine's smells, referred to as the *nose* by the pros. The fruity fragrance of the grape is described as the *aroma,* while the more subtle dusky smell is the *bouquet*, which is the essence of fermentation and aging.

SIP AND SLURP • Your mother said this was bad manners, but it's the best way to taste wine. Take a sip, cradle it on your tongue briefly to warm it, move it around to contact all the taste buds, draw air over it, exhale through your nose, then swallow. This aeration, despite its odd sound, releases the wine's complex flavors. Your taste buds can only detect sweet, sour (acidic), salty and bitter. All the nuances of taste

are in your nose, and mixing air with the wine helps bring out its subtleties. It is said that a good nose can distinguish ten thousand different aromas.

About 50,000 cup-shaped taste buds cover your tongue, and they're grouped together according to their sensory abilities. The sweet receptors are at the tip; the salty ones are behind and along the sides. The sour tasters are toward the back and the bitter ones are behind them, at the tongue's base.

If you'd like to experiment with your taste regions (some of us are easily amused), put bits of sugar, salt, vinegar and other taste sensations on Q-tips. Touch them to various parts of your tongue to see what taste registers where.

What do you look for in the taste of wine? Whites should be fresh and crisp; some will reveal pleasing hints of fruit. The crispness in a wine comes from the acid. Tasters call this the "finish," since that's one of the last things your taste buds pick up as you swallow. A wine too low in acid will be flat and uninteresting; it will have no "finish."

If a wine is off-dry, the taste should not be of sugar or soda pop but delicate, sweet fruit. There should be no cloying aftertaste, which is common in some of those awful pop wines.

Good reds will have a fullness, a mouth-filling "roundness," and taste more like berries than fruit. To me, good reds are more sensuous, since they are warm and mellow to the taste, not crisp and fruity like whites. You know, of course, that some reds will betray a hint of wood, since they're aged in oak barrels to add complexity to their flavor. Chardonnay also may be barrel-aged, adding a nutty, oaky flavor to its lush, fruity taste. An excellent Chardonnay just may be the finest tasting of all wines.

A taste trademark of most reds is tannin, in varying degrees. Tannic acid, as you recall, is leached from the skins and pulp. Justin Meyer explains in *Plain Talk About Fine Wine* than tannin is more of a sensation on the taste buds than a taste. Tannin causes a puckeriness, a subtle rubbery feeling in the mouth. Indeed, it's the substance used to waterproof leather; thus the word "tanning."

When red wines age, tannin molecules are bonded by oxygen, forming chains "that won't fit into the cup-shaped taste bud and thus the wine tastes smoother," says Justin.

Several years ago, when humorist Art Buchwald was invited by the great French winemaker Alexis Lichine to taste a fine Bordeaux, he was instructed to swirl it around in his mouth.

"Clockwise or counterclockwise?" Buchwald asked.

"Clockwise," Lichine replied laconically. "Counterclockwise is for Burgundy."

The wheel

As we've already noted, taste and smell are intertwined. They're focused on a penny-sized patch of olfactory receptors at the back of the nose. Nerve impulses send taste/smell messages to the brain, just a short distance away. The best professional tasters build up an incredible memory bank of taste/smells that helps them identify and separate scores of different wines.

To give serious sniffers and tasters guidance, University of California Professor Ann Noble developed the "Davis Aroma Wheel," which attempts to sort out wine's myriad of aromatic flavors. It begins in the center with basic aromas: chemical, earthy, caramelized, nutty, vegetative, fruity, spicy, floral, microbiological (lactic), oxidized and pungent.

From there, it graduates out to specifics, ranging from burnt toast to hazelnut to butterscotch to coffee. Some aren't very complimentary—tobacco, soapy, fishy and even diesel.

According to Ms. Noble and her wheel, a taster should look for these qualities in specific wines:

Cabernet Sauvignon, Merlot, Malbec and Cabernet Franc: Berry, bell pepper, asparagus, olives, mint, black pepper, vanilla, soy and a buttery essence.

Pinot Noir: Berry, berry jam (strawberry), vanilla and buttery.

Zinfandel: Berry, black pepper, raisins, soy, vanilla and buttery.

Chardonnay: Fruit (apple, peach, citrus, pineapple), spice, cloves, vanilla, buttery.

Sauvignon Blanc: Floral, fruit, (citrus, peach, apricot), spicy, cloves, vanilla, buttery.

White Riesling: Floral, fruit (citrus, peach, apricot, pineapple), honey.

Gewürztraminer: Floral, fruit (citrus, grapefruit, peach), honey, spice.

Chenin Blanc: Floral, fruit (peach, citrus).

Some experts say that Chenin Blanc has the fewest specific characteristics, although we disagree. And why shouldn't we? If everyone agreed at a wine tasting, conversation would be impossible.

Many wine writers insist they can detect cedar, cigar boxes, licorice, pencil shavings, cassis, chocolate, eucalyptus and—good grief!—even the suggestion of a sweaty saddle in wines. Have they run short of adjectives, or had too many samples?

Is it really possible to pick up so many aromas and flavors from a sip of wine? The experts say yes. However, we've never gotten beyond the second rim of the wheel, other than picking up the berry essence of Cabernet, Pinot Noir and Zinfandel, and that tell-tale chili pepper of a Cab.

As in any other attained skill, winetasting requires practice and memory. In wine appreciation classes, instructors often will add a bit of sugar or acid to a wine so it's easily identifiable. They'll then gradually decrease the additives, challenging your smell/taste senses to still find them.

An effective way to practice your sense of smell/taste is to eat or drink something blindfolded, and try to determine what it is. You'll be surprised how much you normally rely on sight and labels to determine what you're tasting. For a fun little test, try it with Jelly Bellies, those tiny jellybeans that come in an alarming range of flavors. Have someone put a few on a plate without telling you what flavors they are. Then, with your eyes closed, pop one in your mouth and try to identify the apricot, cantaloupe, watermelon and other tastes. It's not as easy as you think! (Coffee, lemon and coconut always jump right out, of course.)

Here's a trick to help separate the watermelon flavor from the cantaloupe: give the jelly bean a good workout with your teeth and draw air over the pieces, just as you do in wine tasting.

Judgment day

Once you get into this wine appreciation thing, invite a few friends over for a tasting. You can follow the same techniques and scoring used by professionals who judge wines at competitions.

There are two basic approaches to competitive winetasting: horizontal and vertical. No, horizontal doesn't mean you've tried too many wines. This is a tasting in which the same varietal is sampled from different wineries. In a vertical tasting, you taste wines of the same variety from different vintages.

The most popular scoring system is a twenty-point method developed by U.C. Davis. Our score sheet on the next page is similar to the Davis version, although we've made a few changes to suit our fancy. Note the

MARTIN WINE SCORECARD

Wines:	A	B	C	D	E
APPEARANCE (0-2) Cloudy: 0 Clear: 1 Brilliant: 2					
COLOR (0-2) Off for type: 0 Slightly off: 1 Right on: 2					
AROMA (0-3) Off or weak: 0 Average: 1 Pronounced: 2 Nice bouquet: 3					
ACID (0-2) Bad, vinegary: 0 Slightly off: 1 Right on: 2					
BODY (0-2) Thin, flabby: 0 Slightly wimpy: 1 Right on: 2					
SWEETNESS (0-2) Too high or low: 0 Slightly off: 1 Right on: 2					
FLAVOR (0-3) Abnormal, off: 0 Fair but wimpy: 1 Normal: 2 Right on: 3					
ASTRINGENCY (0-1) Too high or low: 0 Normal: 1					
OVERALL (0-3) Boring, ordinary: 0 Interesting: 1 Provocative: 2 Awesome: 3					
TOTALS (0-20)					

"overall" category at the bottom. Use this to fudge a wine one way or the other, if you like or dislike its overall quality. Like participants in a beauty contest, wines can have nice individual parts, but some are simply put together better than others.

In addition to horizontals and verticals, wine groups conduct competitive tastings to challenge a taster's skill, such as trying to separate a Cabernet from a Pinot Noir from a Zinfandel. Think it's easy? Try it sometime!

A taste of Australia

Which reminds me of the only time I ever scored well at a tasting, although I've taken part in dozens. I flew to Australia several years ago to do a couple of travel stories, including one about the wine country around Adelaide. The plane landed in Sydney and I was greeted by a member of the Australian tourist department, who happened to be a wine aficionado.

I'd just finished a thirteen-hour flight, and both my internal clock and the seasons were reversed, so I was quite spacey. (It was midnight and spring in San Francisco; 11 a.m. and autumn in Australia.)

"You're just in time!" my host said enthusiastically.

"For what?" I blinked sleepily.

"Our wine and food society luncheon. It starts in an

Competitive tastings add an enjoyable dimension to wine appreciation.

hour. I'll drop you at your hotel to freshen up, and pick you up in thirty minutes."

Too polite to refuse my eager escort, I took a quick shower, changed and stumbled downstairs, just in time to be whisked away to the group's gathering at a restaurant.

Prior to lunch, the society conducted a mixed tasting involving four wines: an American Pinot Noir, a French Bordeaux and two Australian Hermitages. (This is a red wine from the Syrah grape, popular in France's Rhône Valley and in Australia.) The competition was two-level: identify the four different wine types and determine which of the two Hermitages was the older.

Perhaps because I was too tired to focus on anything but the wine, I was the only one in the room to score perfectly. My prize, after an hour of winetasting, was a bottle of Champagne. And of course, by Aussie wine club tradition, it was to be opened immediately and shared with my table. This was followed by lunch with more wine and a parade of post-repast ports. At some blurry moment in time, my new Aussie buddies delivered me back to my hotel and poured me into bed.

I awoke with a start at 9 p.m. local time, totally disoriented. I had a prime time hangover and—as my head cleared—a new affection for the outgoing people of Australia. And by the way, they drink three times as much wine as we do, and they make some excellent varieties down there.

Preparing for a tasting

If you decide to host a wine tasting, you can be generous and provide the wines to be sampled, or invite each attendee to bring a bottle.

Preparations for a tasting are simple. Mostly what you need is lots of table space, plenty of glasses and some mildly flavored bread or crackers to clear the palate between sips. Cool water works better, but crackers or little cubes of bread are *très chic*. Make up some score sheets similar to ours, or simply photocopy this one. In a true blind tasting, the wine's identity should be disguised by wrapping bottles in paper bags taped up to the necks, and discarding corks that may carry tell-tale brand names. Then assign a letter or number to each sacked bottle.

Deadly serious tasters never swallow; they taste and then spit to keep their heads as clear as their palates. Thus, a dump bucket is part of the tasting paraphernalia. We certainly expect you and your affable companions to swallow your wines, although a bucket is still a good idea, since some may not want to finish their samples.

With a felt-tipped pen, mark sets of glasses with letters or numbers corresponding with those on your score sheets and the sacked bottles. There should be sufficient glasses available so tasters can have all their wine samples in front of them at the same time for cross-comparisons. (Betty goes back and forth endlessly, comparing the wines in front of her, frowning seriously all the while.)

A tasting requires a startling number of glasses—unless you have only a couple of friends. Please don't yield to the temptation to buy plastic ones! Serious wine shops and most party stores will rent you all the glassware you'll need. Of course, if your guests start doing Russian toasts around the fireplace, you're responsible.

The proper stemware

For your everyday drinking, you'll want the proper glasses. Ignore all that foolishness about using a distinctive shape for each variety of wine.

Through the centuries, specific shapes for both bottles and glasses evolved in different wine producing areas, particularly in France. From these customs has emerged the practice of serving red wine in larger, more globular glasses and whites in smaller, less tapered ones.

However, you need only one basic style for *all* table wines. It should be a tulip shaped glass, since that design directs the wine's aroma and bouquet into your nose. The ideal shape is a fluted tulip, with a round bowl that tapers upward and forms a sort of chimney at the top. The glass should be clear, without bevels or etchings, so you can appreciate the look and color of the wine. It should be large, at least ten ounces. Fill it only a third to a half full, allowing plenty of room for sloshing and sniffing. I like the hefty, comfortable feel of a big, sturdy sixteen-ounce glass in my hand.

The glass should be stout enough to withstand the clinking ritual, and the rousing rinse it will get in the dishwasher. Thin, dainty and fragile crystal glasses just aren't practical for everyday drinking. Incidentally, historians say the custom of clinking wine glasses may have begun in Greece or Rome as a means of signaling the gods, or driving away evil spirits.

Basic table wine glasses are satisfactory for apéritif and dessert wines as well. A sherry gives off its wonderful nutty aroma when properly swirled in a tulip glass; a port will signal its rich treasure of aged grapes in such a vessel. Smaller glasses are acceptable for these wines, since they're served in lesser quantities. If you already have dessert wine glasses, put them to use, but don't make a special trip to the crystal shop.

A lone exception to the single-glass wine service is sparkling wine. It best emits its rising streams of tiny bubbles from long, tapered champagne glasses. Don't use those silly saucers on stems that are common at wedding receptions. They're awkward to handle and their shallow basins encourage the sparkling wine to shed its effervescence too quickly.

The story on storing wine

So now you've really gotten into this thing, and you want to start building a wine collection. Which wines should you buy to "put down," as the connoisseurs say, and where do you put them?

Let's start with the two good reasons for buying wine in quantity:

1: In most areas, you get ten percent off by the case.

2: Some wines improve with age.

Cabernet Sauvignon, of course, is legendary for its ability to benefit from aging. One conjures visions of ancient bottles in darkened cellars, gathering dust and mellowness; subtle flavors marrying in the silence of time. Some Cabs are so "big," say the wine smugs, that they can sleep for decades and still improve. To a lesser degree, full-bodied and high tannin Zinfandel and Pinot Noir—like rare few people—will improve with age. Merlots are already soft and Beaujolais is a light, low-tannin wine best drunk in its youth. Petite Sirah, while ragged at the edges, doesn't seem to improve much through the years; it just becomes dull and boring.

Among the whites, only Chardonnay seems to improve with age, but never for more than a few years.

As you go shopping for wines to "put down," bear in mind that many vintners craft their products to be drunk young, so just any Cab or Zin won't do for the lay-away plan. This is particularly true of large producers that want to keep inventory moving. No offense, Ernest, but we wouldn't go to the Gallo display to stock our wine aging cellar.

You should taste a wine—to find that promising, full-bodied flavor with the sharp edges—to determine if it should sleep in your cellar. That's one of the great advantages of touring the wine country. However, serious wine shops often conduct tastings to help in your selection.

There is at least one other good reason for collecting wines, beyond aging or saving a dime on the dollar. It's nice to have a good selection on hand; to be able to fetch just the right bottle to complement the Foster Farms chicken breast that went on sale at Safeway. And sometimes you feel like a nutty Chardonnay; sometimes you don't.

Cellar dweller?

But suppose you don't have a cellar. Maybe your house is on a concrete slab, or you live on the twelfth floor of a condo complex. You could spend a few thousand dollars on a temperature and humidity controlled wine mausoleum, which would certainly impress your wine smug friends. Or, you could use that money to send your kids to college and still create a safe place for your wines.

Bottles should be stored on their sides to keep the corks moist. They should be in a dark, cool place with little day-to-day temperature variation. Extreme temperature changes cause expansion and contraction, pushing wine out through the porous cork and drawing in air. Remember that wine plus oxygen equals vinegar.

A dark closet on the north side of the house will provide proper protection for your precious wine cache. If your house is on a raised foundation, tuck those puppies beneath the floorboards. An old refrigerator or freezer can serve as a good, inexpensive wine vault. Don't plug it in! You just want to take advantage of its insulation, which will impede daily and seasonal temperature variations.

It's wise to peel the foil caps off the bottles, so you can keep an eye on the corks. If you see discoloration, a sign of leakage around the edges, you'd better schedule that bottle for tonight's dinner.

What price wine?

A good bottle of wine shouldn't cost more than a good bottle of Scotch. Wine is less complicated to produce, and it's taxed at a much lower rate.

So, why are $35 Chardonnays, $45 Cabernets and $125 *Louis Jadot Chevalier-Montrachet Les Demoiselles* on the market? Because people will pay for them. We don't question their motives, but most authors—even clever ones—can't afford such extravagance.

If you follow winetasting results, you'll sometimes note little similarity between quality and price. We regularly discover fine wines for under $15, and even under $10. Only by sampling a variety can you determine which is best for your taste buds and your budget. That's one of the great advantages of going wine country tasting. And if you live far from a wine producing region, inquire at the nearest wine shop about the availability of a local wine club. Such groups often host tastings, inviting members to bring interesting wines.

We don't quarrel with wineries charging startling prices for their products. This is a free market society; let them test the traffic. High prices may reflect the fact that the winery paid top dollar for the finest grapes available, used the best equipment to produce those bottles of wine and "put them down" until they were mature enough to go out on their own. On the other hand, high prices could mean that the vintner borrowed to the hilt to start his boutique winery and he has huge mortgage payments.

Dining with wine

You and your archrival, Watercooler Willie, are being considered for a vice presidency slot. Your boss invites you and your wife out to dinner; the bastard's testing your social graces! He's a wine aficionado but you wouldn't know a Cabernet from a cantaloupe. A guy with a spoon hanging from his vest hands your boss the wine list and—omygawd—he passes it over to you! You quickly realize that you have four choices:

A: Hand it back.

B: Smile bravely at the sommelier and say: "It's difficult to pick from such a wonderful selection. What would *you* suggest?"

C: Order white Zinfandel.

D: Go for it!

You didn't become manager of the Vertical Widget Department through timidity, so you decide to go for it. Here are the five basic steps to bluffing your way through a wine list:

1: Thumb—casually—to the domestic wine section. It's easier to pronounce Zinfandel than *Côtes de Provence Société Civile des Domaines Ott Frères.*

2: Remember the basic guidelines, that—as a general rule—white wines are more suitable with subtly-flavored foods such as poached fish or mildly-seasoned fowl. The flavor of heartier reds will stand up to red meats, highly-spiced dishes and just about anything Italian, up to and including Gina Lolabrigida. (We ignore some of these rules in the third section of this book, but you aren't there yet.)

3: Poll your table to see what's been ordered. If it's a mix of fish and red meat, go for a light red such as a young Zinfandel, or for a more complex white like aged Chardonnay. Resist the temptation to order rosé. Make major points by suggesting that the Chardonnay shouldn't be *too* cold, lest it mask that wonderful spicy aroma. Or be Joe Cool and order a sparkling wine—to celebrate your coming promotion?

4: When the wine arrives, the waiter or sommelier will unplug the bottle and hand you the cork. F'gawdsake, don't sniff it! Check its little bottom to see if it's damp (meaning the wine was properly stored, inverted or on its side), then place it on the table.

5: After the cork business, the waiter will pour a small splash of wine into your glass. Now, here's where you nail down that vice presidency. Swirl it vigorously, keeping the base of the glass on the table so you don't shower the boss. (If you ordered a sparkling wine, you *don't* swirl it, of course.) Then sniff the wine with one long, dramatic inhalation, purse your lips thoughtfully and—don't sip it!* Nod knowingly to the waiter and tell him it's fine.

(* If it's a bad wine, you can tell by the smell. Your nose will advise you if it's starting to spoil, is tainted with sulfur or has a moldy essence from a bad cork. Refuse a wine only if it's spoiled or technically bad; not because you chose poorly and don't care for it.)

The great house wine heist

Do you often order a glass of house wine, because you're dining alone or your partner doesn't drink, and you don't want to tackle a full bottle? Chances are you're being short-changed, particularly if you desire two glasses to get through a meal. House wine is the single greatest profit item of many restaurants.

Let's say you order a jug Cabernet. The restaurant probably paid $6 to $7 wholesale, and it's nicking you $5 a glass. A 1.5-liter bottle contains fifty-two ounces, from which the establishment can get thirteen four-ounce servings. Multiply that by $5 and you've got $65. Not a bad return on the restaurant's investment, but a lousy bargain for you. And if the restaurant is pouring Gallo Hearty Burgundy at five dollars a pop—try not to think about it.

You're better served, literally, by ordering a half-bottle or half carafe if the establishment offers one. That gives you about two and a half glasses. Even if it costs $12 to $14, remember that in the sample above, you paid $10 for two glasses of ordinary wine. If the restaurant sells premium wines by the glass, they may be a better buy than the jug stuff, even for a bit more money. In California and a few other civilized states, the law allows you to take unfinished bottles of wine home, so consider ordering a regular 750 milliliter bottle and asking for a brown paper doggie bag.

Premium wines—full or half bottles—generally are marked up three to five times over wholesale. That's still rather steep, and we think most restaurants charge too much for their wine. But it's better than the ten-fold mark-up on a jug. And by choosing from the full wine list, you'll be getting the wine you like.

Another option, if state laws and the restaurant permit it, is to bring your own wine. (Always check first.) Expect to pay a reasonable corkage fee.

Myth or magic?

We end this section on wine appreciation by demystifying the five most common wine myths.

1: A wine should be allowed to "breathe" before it's served. This ritual—opening a bottle of wine and letting it aerate for an hour or so—is overdone. It's only useful for well-aged reds, to dissipate some of the accumulated vapors that might be negative. However, this can be accomplished simply by giving the wine in your glass a few swirls before your first sip. If the wine is really ancient, with tannin residue at the bottom, you may want to carefully decant it into another container.

2: Laws prohibit adding anything to wine. This is often misunderstood. In California and most other states, wines can't be "ameliorated" to bring up the sugar level, as is often done in France and Germany. However, all sorts of things can be added legally—sulfites to kill wild yeast and inhibit spoilage, various products to clarify a wine, the *dosage* that goes into sparkling wine, natural fruit juices to produce pop wines, herbs and juniper berries to create vermouth, and brandy to produce fortified wines. What *can't* be added to wines in most states are artificial coloring and flavorings.

3: Every year is a "vintage year" in California. Tell that to a grower whose bud set was ruined by a late spring frost, or whose grapes were mildewed by a pre-harvest rain. It is true that the weather is much more stable in California than in France, where "vintage years" are infrequent. However, Mother Nature still has her foul side. What is more likely in California is that bad weather may reduce the yield, although the surviving grapes will be fine. Modern growers can offset much of this weather damage by using frost protection, dusting for mildew and irrigating during a drought. Interestingly, piped-in water is used more often to coat vines with ice as frost protection than to actually irrigate them.

4: Vines have to suffer to produce great grapes. Some wine smugs insist that vines must struggle in poor soil and not be irrigated to yield a premium crop. However, as Amerine and Singleton say in *Wine:*

An Introduction for Americans: "Roots don't care where the water comes from." Further, a lack of nutrients will produce poor grapes, not great ones. What *is* true is that too much water and too many nutrients will promote excessive growth, creating large, lush grapes that will produce thin, watery wine. Grapevines, like people, shouldn't be abused, although they should be challenged in order to yield the best results.

5: *The French produce the best wines because they've been doing it for centuries.* Not so. The commercial wine industry—the ability to produce large amounts of very good wine—really began with the industrial revolution, new cultivation techniques and hygienic discoveries of the nineteenth century. From that standpoint, Americans have been making wine commercially nearly as long as the French. Several regions of America have ideal soil and climate conditions, and its vintners have access to the same skills, discoveries, equipment innovations and educational resources as the Europeans. Indeed, many improvements in cultivation, pruning, vine-training and production have come from American producers and certainly from those two notable California schools of wine—U.C. Davis and Fresno State University.

We have said that the some of the greatest wines come from France. This is true, for French winemakers are as devoted to their craft, as clever and as resourceful as their American counterparts, and perhaps they even put a little soul into their wines. However, to borrow the title from David Darlington's wonderful book tracing the history of Zinfandel, the ultimate French wines come along about as often as angels' visits.

Part II:
THIS HEALTHY BEVERAGE

There is a considerable body of evidence that lower levels of drinking decrease the risk of death from coronary artery disease.

—NATIONAL INSTITUTE ON ALCOHOL ABUSE & ALCOHOLISM

Chapter five

WINE
AND HEALTH
*An old idea whose
time has come*

An old Russian proverb states: "Drink a glass of wine after your soup and steal a ruble from your doctor." In 67 A.D., the Apostle St. Paul recommended using "a little wine for thy stomach's sake." And more than a century ago, Dr. Louis Pasteur called wine "the most hygienic of all beverages."

Obviously, the health benefits of wine aren't new. However, it wasn't until late in the twentieth century that serious studies concerning wine and health began. The flash point came on November 17, 1991, when Morley Safer reported some startling statistics on CBS Television's *60 Minutes* program: Although the French drink nine times more wine than Americans and smoke more cigarettes, they outlive us. This phenomenon was labeled the "French Paradox."

Yet many Americans, perhaps because they're still Puritans at heart, have trouble accepting the idea that anything related to Demon Rum could be good for them. Tasty and relaxing and sensuous and therefore sinful, yes. But healthful? Impossible!

Part of our reluctance to accept this reality stems from the fact that our own government, goaded by an ongoing neo-temperance movement, requires warning labels that: "Consumption of alcoholic beverages...may cause health problems." Despite dozens of studies proving the benefits of moderate drinking, the federal government—at this writing—had refused to edit that message to read: *"Excessive* consumption..."

However, the National Institute on Alcohol Abuse and Alcoholism did grudgingly admit in the early 1990s that moderate drinking may have some positive medical benefits.

As for the American public, if it won't believe reams of evidence, if it won't accept logic, it apparently will believe television. After that *60 Minutes* program revealed that the French pig out on cheese and rich sauces, drink nine times more wine than Americans—mostly red—and still outlive us, a wave of relief swept through the ranks of guilt-ridden wine drink-

> *Americans rushed to their supermarkets to shop for Third World foods, with bottles of wine tucked under their arms.*

ers. Within two weeks of that broadcast, red wine sales jumped forty-four percent. That trend continues to this day. Between 1991 and 1998, sales of red wine in America increased by forty percent, while white wine sales went up only nine percent.

Much of the *60 Minutes* material came from research by Dr. Serge Renaud, head of France's National Health Institute. For several months after the show, this and other studies, which had been ignored by the public, began making front-page headlines. When it was revealed that rural Italians and Greeks often outlive their urban counterparts, and it was suggested that wine, garlic and olive oil were involved, the Mediterranean Diet jumped into the headlines. In droves, Americans rushed to their supermarkets to shop for Third World foods, with bottles of wine tucked under their arms. Of course, holistic health enthusiasts have been proclaiming the benefits of whole grains, pasta and olive oil for decades.

We said in the beginning that this book isn't a health manual. I am not a physician—although my wife and co-author is a doctor of pharmacy, with an extensive knowledge of pharmacology and physiology. I am merely a reporter, guided by experts, gathering facts and sharing the good news about wine and health. Our recommendations concerning wine are intended for healthy individuals who have no problems with alcohol—physiologically or psychologically. If you do not drink, and you have good and proper reasons, by all means don't start on our account.

Drinking is definitely not recommended for those with ulcers or other chronic stomach disorders, liver problems or any internal malfunctions that may be aggravated by alcohol. Further, people on any kind of medication should check with their pharmacist or doctor about a possible negative drug reaction before imbibing.

The good news: For the great majority of Americans who have no problems with alcohol, you've finally found a "sin" that is actually beneficial!

Health, wine and history

None of this news is new, of course. Three decades ago, Dr. Salvatore P. Lucia, professor emeritus of preventive medicine at the University of California's School of Medicine in San Francisco, wrote several books about wine's health benefits. His *Wine and Your Well-Being* is something of a cult classic among wine-and-health enthusiasts. He wrote in 1971:

In diseases of the heart and circulatory system, wine...can provide mild preventive measures against attacks of angina pectoris. Recent studies suggest that wine in the daily diet may act as a protective factor against coronary disease.

If we wanted to hear the good news about wine, we could have started listening centuries ago. Four hundred years before Christ, Hippocrates regarded wine as a medicine. He prescribed it as a dietary beverage, as an agent for cooling fevers, as a purgative and diuretic, and as a dressing for wounds. Since earliest times, physicians have known the value of alcohol as an antiseptic. As in those old Western movies, alcohol was poured both onto and into patients prior to surgery when no anesthetic was available.

Much of the physicians' early respect for wine stemmed from the fact that, in the ancient world of poor sanitation and food spoilage, it was one of the safest things around. Back in 1965, M.A. Amerine and V.L. Singleton, authors of *Wine: An Introduction for Americans,* concluded:

No human pathogens or dangerous food toxin producers occur in wine nor, indeed, would they be likely to survive if deliberately added.

Until World War I, more soldiers died from disease—usually spread through poor sanitation—than from combat. Cyrus the Great, Rome's conqueror of Egypt, kept his troops healthy by ordering them to carry wine in the field to purify local drinking water. Both Greeks and Romans used wine to clean and dress wounds. When St. Paul was quoted in First Timothy (5:23) about using "a little wine," he may have been referring to sanitation, not to digestion. The full quote is: "Drink no longer water but use a little wine for thy stomach's sake."

Within the last few decades, scientists have determined that wine's tannins and other phenolic acids kill many strains of bacteria. They're very effective against those that cause gastro-intestinal diseases. In other words, wine can take vengeance against Montezuma's Revenge.

In our hygienic, sanitized, bottled-water society, infectious diarrhea

When you remove the infant mortality factor, our net lifespan gain after age forty-five is only six years.

isn't exactly a major health concern. What *is* a major concern is that too many Americans die prematurely. Charts show that we gained about twenty-three years in average lifespan in the past hundred years. However, when you remove the infant mortality factor, which was fifteen times greater a century ago than it is today, our net lifespan gain after age forty-five is only *six years*. This despite the fact that we've conquered cholera, smallpox, yellow fever, bubonic plague, typhoid and other killing diseases.

The reason? We've been suffering from a virtual epidemic of heart attacks. In recent years, science has made dramatic strides in discovering the causes, improving intervention procedures and—perhaps most significantly—making Americans cholesterol-aware. We have in fact become zealots. Flooded with information about "good" and "bad" cholesterol, we have rushed to take advantage of the latest cholesterol-reducing agent, be it oatmeal or power-walking.

Even though other nations chide us for our obsession with Quaker Oat Squares and Nautilus machines, all of this health fervor has paid off. Within the past twenty years, America's rate of fatal heart attacks has dropped by thirty percent.

Still, we have a lower life expectancy than many other developed countries. In fact, we're in eleventh place in the industrialized world. The chain-smoking folks of uptight, polluted, industrialized Japan outlive us. So do the laid-back Italians and the haughty French. And some surveys show that subsistence-level Chinese often outlast their Chinese-American relatives.

So we've put down our bowls of oatmeal, loosened the strings on our Nikes and wondered: What's going on here?

Then came Morley Safer and the now-famous *Le Paradoxe Français*. Despite a diet rich in fatty foods and heavy sauces, despite the fact that the average Frenchman's idea of exercise is to reach across the table for another wedge of cheese, they outlive us by about two and a half years. Even more startling, they have *forty percent fewer* heart attacks.

We spend three times as much money per capita on health care as France and most other European nations. In fact, *fifteen cents out of every dollar* goes to medical insurance and health care. We're up to our eyeballs in oatmeal and broccoli; our national heroes are tall black guys in designer tennis shoes who are the epitome of physical fitness; we've built health spas and fat farms from sea to shining sea. Yet, we're still dying at an earlier age than French peasants.

Studies do prove that exercise, lowered cholesterol and moderate wine consumption reduce heart attacks. And we *are* living longer than we did forty years ago.

But, are we living *better*? If so, why do we support so many doctors? Why are American pharmaceutical companies thriving? Why does the cost of health care and health insurance rank third in our household budgets, behind housing and food? Why are so many of our seniors in so-called "convalescent homes?" They're not convalescing but waiting to die, often existing in a vegetative state not much different from the broccoli they were told to eat.

One of our problems, of course, is that not all Americans have caught the health wave. Studies in the late 1990s revealed that *nearly half* of our citizens are overweight. Too many of us are slumping on our couches, watching those tall black guys in tennis shoes perform, instead of getting out and emulating their physical fitness examples. Most fast food chains are little more than cholesterol factories, marketing greasy oversized hamburgers, virtually ignoring their health consequences. Also, many peoples' preoccupation with video games and the internet is generating a new generation of "computer chair potatoes."

Meanwhile, Dr. Renaud, whose studies triggered the French Paradox phenomenon a decade ago, recently completed a new study of 34,000 Frenchmen. The results come as no surprise: Those who drink two to three glasses of wine a day had a thirty percent reduction in death rates from all causes, compared with teetotalers.

In the next chapter, we'll probe more deeply into *Le Paradoxe Français* and find out why those folks break all the health rules and still outlive us. You also will discover that the French, the envy of the gastronomy-wine-and-health world, are picking up some of our bad habits.

Mon dieu!

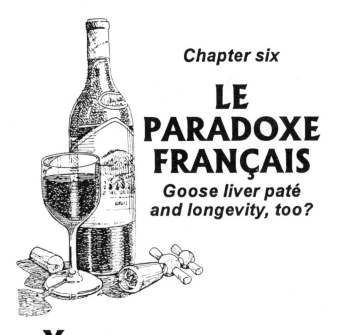

Chapter six

LE PARADOXE FRANÇAIS

Goose liver paté and longevity, too?

You can imagine the stir caused when the French Paradox facts came to light. America's moderate drinkers nodded in eager agreement and neo-prohibitionists cried "foul." The French? They merely smiled and shrugged, as only the French can do, and poured themselves another glass of wine.

France suffers fewer fatal heart attacks than any industrialized nation except Japan. According to World Health Organization figures, the cardiovascular death rate per 100,000 people is 289 in Japan, 310 in France and 464 in the United States.

The paradox goes beyond France's propensity for wine. Studies show that they smoke more heavily, get less exercise, have higher blood pressure and *considerably* higher cholesterol levels than Americans. Yet their heart attack rate is forty percent lower. Further, they live longer and apparently healthier lives. Another curiosity: Their heart disease rate isn't appreciably higher than in southern Mediterranean countries, whose citizens consume much less fat. All this and *foie gras* too? *C'est magnifique!*

Dr. R. Curtis Ellison of the Boston University School of Medicine, who was on that *60 Minutes* show, attributes this apparent contradiction to four major factors:

1: The French eat more vegetables and fruits than we do, usually raw or lightly cooked. Antioxidants found in many vegetables may inhibit cholesterol deposits on arterial walls. Many of these same antioxidants are found in wine, in more concentrated form.

2: Although they consume more fat than Americans, more of it comes from cheese than from meats or whole milk. Animal studies suggest that the fat in cheese, unlike that in milk and other dairy products, binds with calcium and is excreted, rather than being absorbed into the system.

3: The gradual consumption of fats and carbohydrates during their slow, more relaxed meals may affect their absorption and metabolism.

4: Although the French drink more wine than we do, most of it is consumed during meals. Mixing alcohol with food lessens its impact on our innards.

How ironic it may be that the French, who don't share our obsession for counting calories and measuring cholesterol, may be following the proper diet without really trying that hard.

Perhaps the day will come when we Americans shed our preoccupation with calorie and cholesterol counts. Inspired by new dietary logic, we may develop a French appetite for fruits and vegetables, an Italian hankering for pasta and a Greek passion for olive oil. And a little wine with all this? But of course!

And now, the bad news, monsieur

However, with all this good news, trouble may be brewing on the French health horizon. While many publications reporting on the Gaelic paradox view only the bright side, the conservative *Wellness Letter* of the University of California sees potential problems for *La belle France.* An article several years ago suggested that the so-called paradox may be the result of dietary timing, and not some mysterious dietetic contradiction.

A key to cholesterol buildup is the percentage of calories in our diets that comes from saturated fat. The article points out that Americans have been on a high-fat diet for decades, while the French only recently increased their intake of fatty foods, as their economy has improved. The percentage of "fat calories" in the French food supply has increased from twenty-eight percent to nearly forty percent. The current American average is thirty-nine percent, but it has been that high since 1923. Thus, the article suggests that the French may be eating themselves into the same high coronary rate that we now suffer. Also, even though their heart attack rate is relatively low, it's still their leading cause of death.

The death rate from cirrhosis of the liver is twice as high in France as it is in the U.S. In both countries, however, cirrhosis fatalities are rare when compared with heart attacks. According to figures from the World Health Organization, the French death rate per 100,000 is thirty-one for cirrhosis, compared with 310 for cardiovascular causes. In America, it is seventeen compared with 464.

While the *Wellness Letter* article had some valid points, bear in mind that its editors are not exactly friends of wine. Another issue wanted the government to require more detailed warning labels on alcohol containers, including a toll-free number that people can call to learn about alcohol abuse!

Incidentally, despite all this paradoxical excitement, the French drink less than they used to. Their alcohol consumption has been declining steadily for the last fifty years; they drink about thirty percent less per capita than they did in the 1950s. This is not counter to world trends. For decades, drinking has been dropping in most countries, including the U.S. However, sales of premium wines have been increasing. If we're drinking less, at least we're drinking better.

Meanwhile, beware *l'homme de la rue*. With your increase in dietary fat and decline in wine, you soon may be passing us on the health graphs, headed in the wrong direction!

Chapter seven

A CALIFORNIA CURVE?

What the American surveys tell us

Perhaps more significant to Americans than the French Paradox is the J-curve.

Thus far, we've been comparing the lifestyles and eating habits of France to those in America. This chapter will compare Americans to Americans. Scores of domestic studies reveal a fascinating fact: *Moderate drinkers outlive teetotalers.* Some studies also suggest that wine is more effective than other alcoholic drinks in promoting longevity.

The J-curve is a graph line tracing lifespans of abstainers, moderate drinkers and heavy drinkers. It shows that non-drinkers have slightly elevated mortality rates, moderate drinkers have the lowest, and then the line rises sharply for heavy imbibers. Although several wine-and-health studies have focused considerable attention on the J-curve in the past decade, it is not a new concept. The fact that moderate drinkers outlive abstainers was noted by Dr. Raymond Pearl way back in 1926.

We'll call it the "California Curve" since many of the major studies establishing this phenomena were done in that state. An early analysis, conducted over a ten-year period by the Human Populations Laboratory, followed lifestyles and health trends of more than four thousand residents of Alameda, California. It was one of the first studies to reveal that moderate drinkers had a slight longevity advantage over teetotalers.

One of the most comprehensive studies was headed by Dr. Arthur L. Klatsky, chief of the Division of Cardiology at Kaiser Permanente Medical Center in Oakland. His group has been reviewing California drinking habits since the 1970s, and it was one of the first in the state to describe the J-curve. Initial results were published in 1981, based on a ten-year mortality rate for 2,015 Californians. They showed a lower risk of heart attack and longer lifespan for moderate drinkers, when compared with abstainers and heavy drinkers. The J-curve established by Klatsky's observations is shown on the opposite page.

Statistics from a later and more extensive Klatsky study—one of the most comprehensive undertaken by anyone—involved 128,934 adults who were observed for seven years. They had completed detailed medical and lifestyle profiles when they obtained medical insurance coverage from Kaiser Permanente. Since the Kaiser plan provides total health coverage for its members, Dr. Klatsky and his group had an ideal "captive group" to observe.

This study produced the same J-curve as his smaller, more limited review. Even when former drinkers who may have stopped because of health reasons were weeded out from those who had never drunk, the non-drinkers still had more cardiovascular problems and a shorter lifespan than moderate drinkers. That put to rest a theory that non-drinker statistics were skewed because they included one-time heavy boozers or others that abstain because of poor health.

The results also strongly suggested that alcohol wasn't necessarily the primary cause of death among the high risk group. "Heavy drinkers have an increased risk for death from...cirrhosis, motor vehicle accidents, suicide, homicide, certain malignancies and hemor-

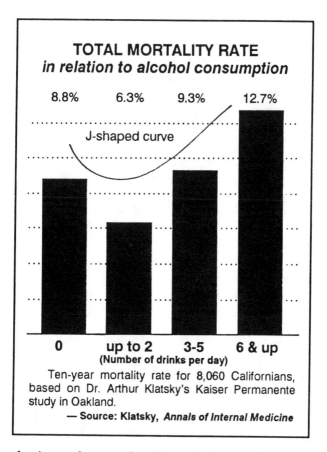

TOTAL MORTALITY RATE
in relation to alcohol consumption

8.8%   6.3%   9.3%   12.7%

J-shaped curve

| 0 | up to 2 | 3-5 | 6 & up |

(Number of drinks per day)

Ten-year mortality rate for 8,060 Californians, based on Dr. Arthur Klatsky's Kaiser Permanente study in Oakland.

— Source: Klatsky, *Annals of Internal Medicine*

rhagic cerebrovascular disease," the report stated. Smoking, common among heavy drinkers, also was a major factor. (The survey was adjusted to account for high mortality rates among smokers.)

How much drink is a drink?

About sixty percent of American adults drink moderately, less than eight percent are considered heavy drinkers and thirty-five percent are abstainers.

What is moderate drinking? Up to two drinks a day, say most health officials. According to a 1999 compilation of fourteen different studies, men who live the longest have just under two drinks per day, while one daily drink appears to be the optimum level for women. As daily alcohol intake increases, the relative death rate for women rises more quickly than for men.

Despite the great variety of drinks available, different beverage servings contain about the same amount of pure alcohol—approximately half an ounce. This is the content of a five-ounce glass of wine, a twelve-ounce beer, three ounces of sherry or port, or a jigger (1.5 ounces) of hard liquor.

Thus, if medical experts recommend no more than two five-ounce glasses of wine a day, that comes to ten ounces. Keep that figure in your head.

The French consume nearly twenty gallons of wine per capita per year, compared with our 2.05. A quick trip to your calculator will reveal that twenty gallons is 2,560 ounces. Divide that by 365 and you get just a tad over seven ounces of wine a day. Moderate drinking, right? But, wait a minute. These are *per capita* figures, including people of all ages. According to surveys, half of France's total population doesn't drink at all. Now we're up to fourteen ounces a day for the wine drinkers, which isn't too much higher than the recommended daily allowance of ten ounces. However, we haven't factored in those who prefer other alcoholic beverages. In fact, the French not only drink more wine, they consume more total alcohol than any other nationality.

French not only drink more wine, they consume more total alcohol than any other nationality.

This would indicate that the French have more than the suggested two-drink-per day limit, while enjoying a longer and healthier lifespan than Americans. Also, in both American and French studies, some observers feel that people may under-report the amounts they drink. (So goes the old joke: "I have only one drink a day—a fifth of Jim Beam.")

"Given that participants in epidemiological studies tend to underestimate their alcohol intake, the actual amounts associated with decreased risk could be somewhat greater," surmised Dr. R. Curtis Ellison, chief of the Department of Preventive Medicine and Epidemiology at the Boston University School of Medicine.

However, we aren't suggesting that you experiment with more than the two-drink recommendation.

J-curve or French curve?

That does bring up some interesting questions, since the French who drink obviously have more than a couple of glasses a day.

Many studies, including Dr. Serge Renaud's French Paradox, indicate that other lifestyle factors also are keys to longevity and good health. They may offset or even complement the effects of several daily drinks. The French are not only living longer; they may be living better. Wine is just part of an overall French-Mediterranean lifestyle that appears to promote good health and longevity. It also includes a diet high in carbohydrates and low in meat protein, and a simpler and less stressful existence.

Dining is less hurried in Mediterranean countries. Instead of counting calories and reading labels, the people treat meals as leisurely social events. Eating on the run is not typical French behavior. Further, studies show that, unlike many Americans, most Mediterraneans do not snack between meals.

The overall diet, in fact, may be more important than so-called "moderate" wine consumption. While the *60 Minutes* episode showed Dr. Renaud enjoying *foie gras* and probably contemplating chocolate *mousse* for dessert, in reality the French diet is high in vegetables, fruits and whole grains.

> *The French are not only living longer; they may be living better.*

It is true that they eat more saturated fats than we do, although their veggie/fruit focus may help offset fat's negative impact.

The Japanese, who out-live us despite a hypertensive lifestyle, follow a low fat, low protein diet high in carbohydrates, mostly from their staple of rice. They consume very little wine, although they do drink green tea, which also has a high level of antioxidents. Succeeding generations of Asian Americans grow taller from their protein-rich Gringo diets, but they tend to have more health problems and a shorter lifespan than their homeland kin.

Also, body weight may be a key factor. America is indeed the land of the fat. Any trip to the supermarket will tell you that. And a trip overseas will reveal that chubbiness is primarily an American phenomenon. Betty and I have traveled extensively, and have noted that obesity—common in America—is rare overseas. Women in many countries attain that "matronly look" in their middle years, but very few are grossly fat.

Although Americans talk a good line about healthy eating, recent studies reveal that nearly half of our adult population is overweight. Too many of us subsist on diets of protein-rich, calorie-rich, cholesterol-rich, carbohydrate-poor processed foods. Most fast foods are notoriously high in fat, salt and sugar.

> **"Increased longevity of wine drinkers may be more attributable to the lifestyle of the wine drinker than to the wine itself."**
> —Dr. Arthur L. Klatsky

Another factor in the French-American paradox is the pattern of consumption. Even though the French drink nine times more wine than we do and twice as much total alcohol, alcoholism is much more common in America. (However, different diagnostic standards may push our rate of alcoholism higher that in some other countries.)

Although our J-curve swings upward sharply with increased alcohol consumption, it's likely skewed by other factors. Most alcoholics are heavy smokers, their diets are poor and they get very little exercise. Also, surveys have shown that binge drinking is more common in America. Fourteen drinks a week may be good for you, but not if you take them all at one sitting!

Is it the wine, or the good life?

Although this book is about wine, and we are wine advocates, it is obvious that the essence of the grape is only one factor in longevity, and perhaps not the primary one. We must grant major credit to overall lifestyle, and certainly to a good diet.

This was strongly indicated in the Klatsky study. In addition to the fact that moderate drinkers in California outlive teetotalers and heavy drinkers, it revealed that wine drinkers lead healthier lives than other people. They smoke less, exercise more, are less likely to be overweight and follow better diets than either abstainers or chronic boozers. They also are better educated and more affluent.

"Increased longevity of wine drinkers compared to beer or liquor drinkers may be more attributable to the lifestyle of the wine drinker than to the wine itself," commented Dr. Klatsky. "We really have to interpret (our findings) in light of the fact that...wine drinkers in California are a health-conscious lot, who engage in a healthy lifestyle in various ways."

Another point: when wine is consumed, it's often done under relaxed social conditions, as it is in France. Surveys show that seventy-five percent of wine drinking in America takes place in the home, and eighty-two percent of that occurs during mealtime. Wine is not America's beverage of choice for the power lunch.

These findings tend to agree with French revelations, that moderate drinking is only part of a healthy lifestyle. Dr. Andrew Waterhouse of the University of California at Davis, a leading authority on wine and antioxidants, points out:

What's important about the leisurely French lunch is that the stress level of the work day gets a break. And having a glass of wine or a beer when one gets home at the end of the day is a great stress reducer.

Obviously, alcohol is delivering both physiological and psychological benefits to the body. Physicians have long recognized that a positive attitude and feeling of well-being are important factors in health. So, which is the cause and which is the effect? It would appear that they are part of an overall package that includes moderate drinking, good health practices and a healthy outlook on life.

Wine drinkers: an American profile

Curious to find a profile of the typical American wine-lover, sociologists David Pittman and Hugh Klein of Washington University in St. Louis studied our drinking habits for five years. They determined that forty-three percent of all adult Americans drink some kind of alcohol at least once in any given week. (Other studies put the figure as high as sixty percent.)

Their survey showed that wine-drinking tends to peak in the middle years, from age forty-five to sixty-four. Groups on both sides of that range reported

How long they live;
How much wine they drink

These are the top twenty nations in overall lifespan, with their worldwide rank in wine consumption per capita. You will note that many countries using very little wine are quite high in life expectancy.

COUNTRY	LIFESPAN	WINE RANK
1. Japan	78.9	40
2. Sweden	77.6	21
3. Switzerland	77.4	6
4. Netherlands	77.0	19
5. Austria	77.0	8
6. Norway	76.6	31
7. Canada	76.4	26
8. France	76.2	1
9. Germany	75.5	12
10. Iceland	75.5	n/a*
11. United States	75.4	29
12. Finland	75.0	28
13. Denmark	74.9	13
14. United Kingdom	74.8	25
15. New Zealand	74.6	23
16. Greece	74.3	9
17. Israel	73.9	33
18. Spain	73.6	7
19. Italy	73.3	3
20. Australia	73.2	18

*Although we could not find a specific ranking for wine consumption in Iceland, it is very low, on a par with most Scandinavian countries.

drinking wine less frequently. As with Dr. Klatsky's California study, the Pittman-Klein review revealed that wine drinking was most popular for the well-educated middle to upper income class. More than sixty percent of the imbibers had attended graduate school, and more than half had household incomes nearly double the U.S. average.

Unlike the French, who often drink wine for both lunch and dinner, Americans use it primarily as an evening ritual. Only nine percent of those surveyed by doctors Pittman and Klein said they drank wine before 3 p.m. Fifty-eight percent said they did most of their wine drinking on weekends, compared with forty-two percent on weekdays. Like the French, most American wine drinkers in the survey did their sipping at home. Not surprisingly, when they drank away from home, it was usually at restaurants with meals.

Who lives the longest?

Although wine drinkers clearly have fewer heart attacks than abstainers, when you look at total longevity on the chart on the opposite page, wine's role appears to be less significant. In fact, going north to south in Europe, you see a reverse effect. The heavy wine drinkers of France, Italy and other Mediterranean regions have fewer heart problems, but most northern Europeans have slightly longer lifespans. The lone exception is Switzerland, ranking third in overall longevity and sixth in wine consumption. That small country's good economy and excellent health facilities may help account for its dual high ranking.

Any of the three primary factors—moderate drinking, good diet or low-key lifestyle—seems capable of taking the lead in promoting health and longevity.

Ten keys to a healthy lifestyle

Achieving the "good life" requires a little effort. What follows is a summation of what we have learned from several months of study about wine consumption, diet, health and lifespan. Our ten pointers are not listed in any particular order of importance. The medical community is still mixed on assigning levels of credit for these various elements of "living right."

1: Follow a diet high in complex carbohydrates (rice, breads, pastas, lentils), plus lots of fruits and vegetables.

2: Limit your intake of protein, particularly from red meats.

3: Use skim milk instead of whole milk.

4: Use vegetable oil (preferably olive oil) instead of animal fat for cooking.

5: Avoid obesity. Most obese people get that way by following health-threatening diets that are high in cholesterol and saturated fats.

6: Drink one or two glasses of wine a day, preferably with meals. (Some studies indicate that other alcoholic beverages are as effective as wine in promoting longevity.)

7: Relax more at meals; eat at a leisurely pace and avoid between-meal snacks.

8: Get more exercise. Couch potatoes don't live longer; it just *seems* longer.

9: Don't smoke. Tobacco smoke is the single most damaging thing many people put into their bodies. The American Heart Association calls smoking the *primary* factor in heart disease. Although anti-alcohol groups like to quote figures about the costs of alcoholism, the cost of treating disease-ridden smokers is much higher. About eighteen million Americans are alcoholics, but *forty million* are smokers. In fact, the great majority of alcoholics also smoke, which invariably skews health statistics about heavy drinkers.

10: Spend less time worrying about life and more time enjoying it.

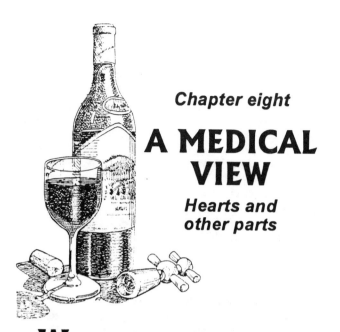

Chapter eight

A MEDICAL VIEW

*Hearts and
other parts*

We now know that at least three elements can work together to promote good health and longevity: lifestyle, overall diet and the physiological and psychological benefits of moderate drinking.

The role of wine as a medical tool has been known for centuries, as we noted earlier. Some of its value was more folklore than fact, however. In ancient Egypt, it was mixed with honey as an enema and one early physician extolled its ability to "regulate the urine, cause purgation, kill tapeworm, relieve anorexia, insomnia and all diseases marked by cough."

Today, of course, fact has been separated from fiction. In this chapter, we discuss wine's role in personal health. We begin with the heart of the matter, since that's getting most of the attention.

All about cholesterol

A decade ago, most of us couldn't even spell "cholesterol." Now, it is a favorite buzz-word of health enthusiasts. To comprehend the wine-and-health findings of the past decade, we must understand what cholesterol is and what it does.

First, it's not a foreign substance in our bodies. It's a naturally-occurring waxy compound, manufactured by the liver, used in building cell membranes and hormones, and it helps the body produce vitamin D. Our liver is capable of producing all the cholesterol our system requires. When we eat virtually any animal or dairy food, we take in "dietary cholesterol." The combined total that shows up in our bloodstream is called "serum cholesterol."

Although cholesterol molecules use the bloodstream for passage, they're insoluble because of their waxy makeup. Their mass transit system is provided by *lipoprotein,* a soluble protein molecule that embraces cholesterol and serves as a sort of water taxi. It is the *density* of this carrier that gives us problems, not the cholesterol itself.

Good guys and bad guys

High density lipoprotein (HDL) and low density lipoprotein (LDL) are the key players in the cholesterol drama. When body cells have too much cholesterol, HDL—the good guy—carries the excess to the liver, where it is converted into bile salts and excreted. On the other hand, LDL—the villain of the piece—picks up cholesterol from the liver and delivers it to cells that need it. When cells become saturated with cholesterol, LDL circulates aimlessly through the bloodstream, looking for a place to unload its cargo. In its wanderings, the cholesterol begins to oxidize and deteriorate; some of the "damaged" cholesterol is deposited on arterial walls. A frightening word enters our medical vocabulary—*arteriosclerosis.*

This is a narrowing of arterial walls by a build-up of cholesterol deposits. When the heart's own arteries are restricted but not completely blocked, the *myocardium* or heart muscle starts sending pain messages because it isn't getting enough oxygen-carrying blood. This is *angina pectoris*, that sharp pain or tight-fisted feeling in the chest. When an artery in the heart is completely blocked, perhaps by a floating blood clot or even a chunk of dislodged cholesterol plaque, a *myocardial infarction* or heart attack occurs. It's also called a *coronary thrombosis*, a reference to the coronary artery and *thrombus,* a medical term for clot.

Tragically, for nearly a third of heart attack victims, the first and final symptom is death. Cardiovascular problems affect thirty percent of American men and ten percent of women before they reach age sixty. Fortunately, they're not always fatal.

Although heart-related deaths have dropped by nearly a third in the past twenty years, they still kill nearly 600 thousand Americans annually, accounting for almost half of all deaths. Our overall death rate is about 1,060 per 100,000 people. Of these, 464 are from coronaries, 246 from cancer, seventeen from cirrhosis and 137 from accidents.

Even with the decline in lethal coronaries, cardiovascular diseases cost the American people more than $117 billion a year, reports the American Heart Association. Quoth Dr. Edward S. Cooper, AHA president:

Because of these high costs...it's time all Americans take what responsibility they can to lower their risk of cardiovascular disease. This means learning about major modifiable risk factors for heart disease and stroke—high blood pressure, high blood cholesterol, cigarette smoke and physical inactivity, and taking steps to correct them.

In recent years we have become obsessed—and rightly so—with our cholesterol count, which is measured as milligrams per deciliter of blood. Medical specialists send us mixed messages as to the ideal level, although most agree with National Institute of Health guidelines, that it should be under 200. Some physicians say it should be under 180.

> **In recent years we have become obsessed with our cholesterol count.**

The average cholesterol count for American men thirty-five and older ranges from 200 to 215; for women it's 185 to 230. Although 240 and above puts men in the high risk group, bear in mind that many men with cholesterol counts in the low 200s develop coronary heart problems. Women usually have lower cholesterol levels and lower incidence of heart problems until menopause, then their levels begin to elevate. Their risks of heart problems rise with their post-menopausal cholesterol rates.

A third element in cholesterol is triglycerides, another fatty substance produced by the liver; it helps build cell walls. Again, your body produces all you need, and an elevated triglyceride level also appears to cause arterial clogging. Unlike cholesterol, triglycerides occur in both animal and plant material, so even a vegetarian can have high triglyceride levels, particularly from ingesting excessive saturated vegetable oils. Further, your liver will convert excess calories from fats, sugar and alcohol into triglycerides.

Even more important than your total cholesterol count is your ratio of high density lipoprotein to total cholesterol, since HDL prevents arteriosclerosis while LDL promotes it. Thus, a healthy cholesterol count should be high in HDL and low in both LDL and triglycerides. Very low density lipoprotein (VLDL) is the triglyceride water taxi. When figured into your cholesterol count, the VLDL measure will be a fifth of your total triglycerides, since these capsules are about one-fifth cholesterol.

If you have a cholesterol check, the printout may read this way:

HDL	50
LDL	150
VLDL	25 (one-fifth of 125)
Total	225

To find your HDL/cholesterol ratio, divide the total cholesterol count by the HDL level. In our sample, 225 divided by fifty equals 4.5. The average for American men is five. Ideally, it should be lower, preferably under four. The odds of getting a heart attack are cut in half if you can lower your HDL/cholesterol ratio from five to 3.3. Vegetarians often get below three.

Protecting your heart

The Johns Hopkins Medical Letter, *Health After 50,* lists these steps that individuals can take to reduce their heart attack risk. They were compiled from reviews of 200 separate studies.

1: Stop smoking or never start. This cuts the risk of heart problems by fifty to seventy percent.

2: Reduce cholesterol levels. For every one percent reduction in serum cholesterol, the risk of heart problems declines two to three percent.

3: Lower your blood pressure. Hypertension can be eased with a blend of diet and drug therapy. Heart attack risks decrease two to three percent with each one-point reduction in diastolic blood pressure.

4: Get more exercise. Studies show a forty-five percent reduction in heart problems for those following an active lifestyle, compared with sedentary folks.

5: Keep your body weight down. People who are obese (more than twenty percent above normal weight) have a thirty-five to fifty-five percent greater risk of heart problems. Some studies indicate that it's not the added pounds themselves, but the factors that put on those pounds, such as a high-fat diet, high cholesterol count and sedentary lifestyle. Excess body weight makes exercise difficult and uncomfortable.

6: Use alcohol moderately. A review of the various alcohol-and-health studies indicates a twenty-five to forty percent lower risk of heart attacks among those who have one to two drinks a day, compared with non-drinkers.

7: Take a low aspirin dose, under medical supervision. Some studies show that an aspirin tablet every day or every other day reduces coronary heart problems by thirty-three percent. Ingredients in aspirin inhibit blood clotting. Do the aspirin thing only under medical supervision, since it causes minor stomach bleeding and may have other side effects.

8: For diabetics: maintain a stable blood sugar level. This is difficult, since a diabetic's glycemic level rises and falls dramatically between insulin shots. Studies have shown that a carefully regimented diet and more precise monitoring of insulin doses during the day helps diabetics avoid heart disease and other medical problems. Recent improvements in blood sugar monitoring devices are helping diabetics lead healthier lives.

Wine's role in prevention

It's well established that wine and other alcoholic beverages reduce the likelihood of a "coronary event." But how? Several elements appear to be involved:

Increasing HDL: Research at Harvard's School of Public Health has determined—along with several other studies—that wine and other alcoholic drinks increase the HDL count. The Harvard study indicated that a one-point increase in HDL produced a seven percent reduction in heart attacks.

Lowering LDL: Moderate drinkers may get a double bonus, since alcohol also appears to reduce LDL levels. The famous Framingham Heart Study, a forty-year observation of the citizens of Framingham, Massachusetts, found that the risk of heart attack rises two percent for every one percent increase in "bad" cholesterol levels above 150. The study found *no heart attacks* among those with cholesterol levels below 150.

Decreasing blood clotting: Many scientists feel that wine has an anti-clotting action, like aspirin. Foods rich in lipids (fatty, non-water-soluble substances) tend to promote blood clotting. Wine taken with meals may counteract this action, suggests Dr. Renaud of France's national health institute.

Reducing stress: Wine's sedative capabilities may help ease stress-related coronary artery spasms.

Preventing LDL oxidation: This may be a key factor in avoiding heart disease. We've saved it until last only because it requires a bit of explaining. Much of the laboratory exploration in this area was accomplished by Dr. Andrew L. Waterhouse and others at the University of California at Davis.

Oxidation occurs when oxygen combines with a substance to form a new compound, such as the conversion of iron to iron oxide (rust), and changing wine to acetic acid (vinegar). When oxidation occurs in the bloodstream, oxidants called free radicals are released. These can damage cholesterol, arterial walls, cell membranes, other tissues and possibly DNA—the strung-together links of your genetic legacy. Studies indicate that the oxidation or damaging of low density cholesterol contributes to plaque build-up.

"Damaged LDL settles in arterial walls, where it in turn damages the artery," said the Dr. Waterhouse. "Macrophages and other repair particles start gathering at this site, absorb the damaged LDL, and a buildup of plaque begins."

The Davis group has confirmed what other scientists had suspected—that tannin compounds in red wine work to inhibit LDL oxidation. These elements have been identified as phenols and the list is quite extensive, including *resveratrol, epicatechin* and *quercetin*. Resveratrol, an ingredient also found in herbal Japanese and Chinese folk medicine, apparently is produced by grapes to fight plant disease. *Quercetin* and *epicatechin* are compounds common to many fruits and vegetables in addition to grapes.

The antioxidant action of phenols was proven *in-vitro* (in the lab) in experiments conducted by Dr. Waterhouse, the late Dr. John E. Kinsella and others. When phenolic compounds from red wine were added to LDL taken from human blood samples, oxidation was inhibited by sixty to ninety percent.

"We looked at three phenol compounds in wine in our test and found all of them to be more potent than vitamin E in preventing oxidation of LDL," said Dr. Waterhouse. "And vitamin E is associated with a reduction in heart disease."

Two recent studies, one at a laboratory in Cambridge, England, and one by physicians in Japan, also demonstrated that red wine inhibited LDL oxidation.

Incidentally, antioxidants also exist in fresh fruits and vegetables, particularly blueberries.

Red wine or Johnny Walker Red?

An argument continues among scientists as to whether the essence of the grape is more effective in preventing heart problems than other alcoholic beverages. Results of studies tend to be mixed, although some tilt slightly in favor of wine.

Dr. Renaud's group in France and others champion red wine because of its anti-clotting actions and antioxidant phenols. And certainly research at U.C. Davis points to its ability to prevent LDL oxidation. However, different studies suggest that other drinks work as well. Elements in alcohol itself may inhibit clotting, and tests do show that alcohol lowers LDL counts.

A recent survey of 128,934 adults conducted at the Kaiser Permanente Medical Center in Oakland, California, favors wine and beer, although only slightly. And in this survey, red wine fared no better than white. The study, led by Dr. Arthur Klatsky and published in *Excerpta Medica* concluded:

Drinking ethyl alcohol apparently protects against coronary disease, and there may be minor additional benefits associated with drinking both beer and wine, but not especially red wine. (© 1997 by *Excerpta Medica*)

The Harvard School of Public Health, observing the lifestyles of 44,000 male health professionals, found that those who had up to two drinks a day had a twenty-six percent lower chance of developing heart disease than those who had less than half a drink. Most participants in that study drank whiskey.

An earlier study by Dr. Klatsky's group found that white wine drinkers fared slightly better than those who prefer red wine or other types of alcohol. (Sorry about that, Dr. Renaud.) "Wine preference (both red and white) was associated with significantly lower relative risk for cardio-vascular death" when compared with hard liquor, according to his study. However, the study "found no significant relation of beverage preference to mortality from all causes of death."

> *"Although the evidence is not conclusive, more and more studies point to very positive benefits from wine's phenolic compounds."*
>
> — Dr. Andrew Waterhouse

In a large study concluded about ten years ago, the American Cancer Society followed the lifestyles and health problems of 275,000 middle-aged men for a dozen years. The results: those who took one or two drinks a day had twenty percent fewer heart problems than teetotalers. Those participants drank a variety of alcoholic beverages. Out in the Pacific, the Honolulu Heart Study found that male Japanese-Hawaiians who took three to six drinks a week had a heart disease rate of three percent during the six-year term of the study, compared with five percent for abstainers. And the drink of choice in this study? Beer, bruddah.

"Although the evidence is not conclusive, more and more studies point to very positive benefits from wine's phenolic compounds," Dr. Waterhouse said.

We'll side with the grape as well. You'll note that this tome is entitled *The Ultimate **Wine** Book,* so there's no secret to the site of our sympathies. Certainly, no study has suggested that Jack Daniels or Primo Beer is *superior* to Zinfandel in preventing heart disease.

And as the French are telling us, wine is not only a convivial drink, it is an essential part of dining. Can you imagine *Coquilles St. Jacques* with scotch and soda?

Other wine and health aspects

Alcohol's role in other health areas is mixed. In most situations, moderate drinking is a neutral factor; in some, it's beneficial. In all cases, excessive drinking, and the smoking-malnutrition-tension baggage that it carries, is damaging.

CANCER: No studies have proven that alcoholic beverages help prevent cancer in humans. However, experiments have shown that—in the laboratory at least—elements in red wine can inhibit cancer cell growth. Further, no studies have shown that moderate drinking *contributes* to cancer's development.

"Alcohol appears to have a relatively small impact on the total occurrence of cancer," says the American Council on Science and Health. "For this reason, an anti-alcohol campaign for the prevention of cancer is not considered to be justified." ACSH says it neither recommends nor condemns the use of alcohol, but provides guidelines for those who choose to drink. So we can assume the cancer comment is without bias.

Although the jury is still out on cancer and alcohol, recent studies have produced some interesting results. France's largest wine-and-health survey, involving 34,000 men, showed a *nineteen percent* reduction in cancer risk for moderate drinkers, compared with non-drinkers. The study, concluded in the late 1990s, was led by none other than Dr. Serge Renaud.

Results of other surveys through the years are mixed, from slight reductions in cancer rates among moderate drinkers to none at all. Abuse of alcohol has been linked to cancer, although this may be related to the fact that most alcoholics are heavy smokers.

Two recent studies, one using lifestyle data and the other employing lab tests, indicated that elements found in red wine may inhibit cancer growth in humans. Danish researchers, drawing on data from the

Copenhagen City Heart Study, concluded that those who drank from one to three glasses of wine a day were at a slightly lower risk of getting upper digestive tract cancer. In lab tests, a team of researchers at the University of Illinois noted that resveratrol inhibited the activity of a gene that has been associated with the growth of cancer tumors.

In tests conducted at the University of California at Berkeley by biochemist Dr. Terrance J. Leighton, the antioxidant quercetin inhibited the conversion of normal cells to cancer cells. This compound exists in a variety of plant foods, although it isn't activated until the final stages of digestion, by enzymes in the lower colon. However, quercetin in wine is activated by fermentation, so it apparently goes to work much earlier in the digestive process.

Attempts to induce cancer in laboratory mice by keeping them juiced haven't met with much success. Even after the critters were fed the human equivalent of four bottles of whiskey a day for life, the studies "failed to support a conclusion that alcohol is carcinogenic at any level," said Dr. Emanuel Rubin of the Jefferson Medical College in Philadelphia.

Dr. Marvin Goldman, professor of toxicology at U.C. Davis, agreed: "The overwhelming and consistent trend in the laboratory experiments is that alcohol is not a carcinogen."

On the other hand, results of experiments published in the *American Journal of Clinical Nutrition* recently revealed that mice fed wine solids with the alcohol removed were free of cancer tumors forty percent longer than other mice.

STROKES: These occur either when a blood vessel in the brain bursts (hemorrhagic) or when it's blocked (occlusive). Dr. Klatsky's Kaiser Permanente group found no increase in hemorrhagic strokes when comparing light drinkers (up to two a day) with non-drinkers, but a thirty-eight percent increase among those having three or more drinks a day. This also has been observed in the so-called "aspirin therapy," since both aspirin and alcohol inhibit clotting that might seal the rupture. However, since heart attacks are ten times more common that strokes, this appears to be a favorable trade-off. Not surprisingly, moderate drinking provided considerable protection against the more common occlusive strokes in Dr. Klatsky's studies.

CIRRHOSIS: Studies show that only a very high intake of alcohol leads to liver damage. The American Council on Science and Health suggests that the risk is great only if a person drinks heavily over an extended period. Cirrhosis, incidentally, is not a disease but a scarring of the liver which prevents it from functioning. Tobacco tars are particularly hard on the liver, so again we see that drinking-smoking combination among alcoholics. Studies show that women who drink

> *Statistically, cirrhosis of the liver is an illusive target as far as alcohol is concerned.*

heavily are more susceptible to liver damage than men, even beyond the difference in their comparative body weights.

Cirrhosis is an illusive target as far as alcohol is concerned. Japan has a higher cirrhosis rate than the United States, although per capita alcohol consumption is less. The Irish drink as much alcohol as Americans and their cirrhosis rate is only one-fourth ours. Even more curious, the cirrhosis rate in France—twice that of America—is lowest in rural wine-drinking areas and highest in urban hard liquor and beer areas.

STRESS: A study by the Alcohol Research Group in Berkeley, California, reported that moderate drinkers have fewer problems with stress and depression than abstainers and heavy drinkers. Whether this is a cause or an effect is unclear. People leading full, productive lives drink to relax; those unhappy with their lot drink to forget. It's well established that most alcoholics have very low self esteem and often suffer depression. It also could be suggested that uptight, stressed personalities tend to be abstainers—a kind of Puritan syndrome. However, we're not aware of any clinical evidence of this.

HYPERTENSION: A close cousin of stress but not directly related, hypertension is a major player in the heart attack arena. A 35-year-old male with blood pressure around 142 is twice as likely to suffer a heart attack within twenty years as one whose pressure is under 120. Wine can play a significant role in blood pressure levels. One or two drinks elevates pressure about 1.6 points. After six drinks, it's elevated by 5. Thus three or more drinks a day increases the risk of hypertension, and six or more doubles that risk. Blood pressure of moderate drinkers returns to its original range shortly after drinking stops. It's interesting, from a curiosity standpoint, that the calming effect of a drink elevates blood pressure. Another curiosity: women's blood pressure is less affected by alcohol than men's.

DIABETES: The risk of developing adult-onset diabetes may be as much as thirty percent lower among moderate drinkers than abstainers, according to four different studies. Scientists don't yet know why.

HEADACHES: Those fearsome headaches that accompany a hangover suggest that alcohol, or at least some ingredient in alcoholic beverages, are to blame. Even some moderate drinkers report suffering minor headaches after imbibing, particularly drinkers of red wine. Some doctors and dietitians have suggested that the astringent effect of tannin may be the culprit.

There are many different causes of headaches, ranging from tension to sinus congestion to allergies. Some specialists suspect that caffeine, or perhaps caffeine withdrawal, may be a headache producer.

ANTI-BACTERIAL ACTION: Polyphenols in wine are effective killers of bacteria and even some viruses. Tests led by Dr. Martin Weisse at West Virginia University demonstrated that both red and white wine killed bacteria that can cause food poisoning, dysentery and diarrhea. Researchers said it outperformed the ingredients in PeptoBismol and it was more effective than tequila. Researchers didn't say why tequila was used, although it is a product of Mexico, where visitors sometimes suffer stomach distress. Presumably, the message is: Drink wine, not margaritas.

In a pinch, wine can help purify drinking water, but don't rely on it in areas with poor sanitation since it may not kill *all* harmful bacteria. (Just drink the wine itself, or the local beer.) Some lab tests suggest that wine concentrates help clear up herpes infections, although this hasn't been studied extensively.

In 1892, a Paris physician noted that wine drinkers were less likely to be stricken during a cholera epidemic, so he advised mixing wine with drinking water. An Austrian military doctor named Alois Pick put this to the laboratory test and found that wine, even in diluted amounts, did indeed kill cholera and typhoid bacteria. The antiseptic value of wine was a key element in Dr. Louis Pasteur's experiments.

Apparently, fermentation activates or liberates wine's bacteria-killing action, since it's more effective than grapes or grape juice.

WEIGHT GAIN: Although wine is high in calories, it doesn't appear to contribute to weight gain or body fat buildup, according to a study done in the late 1990s. In the experiment, conducted by Dr. Loren Cordain at the Department of Exercise and Sports Science at Colorado State University, two glasses of wine were added to the daily diet of the test subjects. After six weeks, they had no increase in weight or body fat, despite the additional calories. A much larger Finnish study involving drinking habits of 27,215 middle-age men in-

> *Scientists aren't quite sure why wine calories don't wind up on your waistline.*

dicated that moderate drinkers tend to be leaner. Although those studies are rather new, experiments conducted in the 1980s by California's Stanford University had the same result. Several overweight men were given two glasses of wine with dinner and they gained no weight. They even ate more food, since wine is known to be an appetite stimulant.

Scientists aren't quite sure why wine calories don't wind up on your waistline. They may be metabolized differently than other calories, and of course they contain no fat content or cholesterol. The Stanford study did report that wine drinkers' basal metabolism rate increased, and that burns off more calories.

In case you're curious, a five-ounce serving of table wine has about 100 calories and sweet dessert wines have twice that amount. Twelve ounces of regular beer contains 150 calories and light beer has one-third less. Most eighty-proof liquor has around 100 calories per

1.5 ounces. Surprisingly, demon rum has only about seventy calories, despite the fact that it's distilled from sugar cane.

GERIATRIC HEALTH: Many doctors prescribe moderate amounts of wine for seniors, unless other medical conditions preclude its use. It builds lagging appetites, aids digestion, boosts spirits and serves as a mild tranquilizer for sleep. Studies also suggest that a little wine is good for the mind. "Moderate drinking seemed to improve memory, problem solving and reasoning ability," said Jean Carper, author of the book *Stop Aging Now!* A noted nutritionist, she compiled results from several studies on wine and geriatric health. She said drinking wine with meals was the seniors' "best anti-aging bet."

> *Many doctors prescribe moderate amounts of wine for seniors.*
> *It builds lagging appetites, boosts spirits and serves as a mild tranquilizer.*

With regard to senior sipping, the American Council on Science and Health has written:

Studies of the therapeutic effects of modest amounts of beer or wine added to the evening meal of elderly patients have shown that (they) displayed a significant increase in contact with each other and the staff, a reduction of incontinence and an impressive reduction in the need for prescribed psychotherapeutic drugs. Patients who received some alcoholic beverages showed functional improvements in comparison to (those) who were given non-alcoholic beverages in a similar setting.

Nearly thirty years ago, Dr. Salvatore Lucia, author of *Wine and Your Well-Being*, noted similar benefits:

The infirmities of old age often call for bland and uninteresting foods at a time when the digestive system is becoming less efficient. The presence of wine helps brighten such a dreary table. Wine's composition bears a close resemblance to gastric juice and aids in digestion. While wine is no panacea for hypertension, its sedative properties lessen the pressure brought on by emotional factors, and the peace of mind which may significantly prolong a useful life.

Further, he wrote, wine's dilating effect helps circulation to the extremities, which often is a problem for seniors. Thus, it can warm the hands and feet as well as the heart.

Doctors do caution that the elderly metabolize alcohol more slowly, so moderation is important. Further, alcohol-drug interactions are more likely because many seniors are on a variety of medications.

ALZHEIMER'S DISEASE AND DEMENTIA: A recent survey of 3,700 men and women in France, aged sixty-five and older, indicated that moderate wine drinkers had a seventy-five percent decrease in the rate of Alzheimer's and an eighty percent decrease in dementia, compared with abstainers. The survey was conducted by Dr. Marc Orgogozo of Hospital Pellegrin in Bordeaux. A study seven years earlier, involving the same group, showed that moderate wine drinkers performed cognitive functions better than non-drinkers.

Only limited research has been done in this area, and scientists still aren't sure how wine effects mental function in seniors. However, Dr. Orgogozo, who led both studies, concluded: "Wine consumption remains one of their last pleasures in this stage of life; our findings argue against prohibiting mild or moderate wine consumption in the elderly."

LEAD IN WINE: Many foods, including wine, contain trace amounts of lead, although they are far below levels considered harmful by the Food and Drug Administration. The FDA would like lead levels in food kept below 300 parts per billion. Lab studies of California wine showed an average of twenty-one PPB. That's the same as chocolate chip cookies, about half the amount in fresh or frozen spinach and one third the level in spaghetti with meat sauce.

Since lead-tin foil wraps were traditionally used to cover bottle tops until the early 1990s, both the FDA and wine industry recommend removing the foil completely, pulling the cork and then wiping the neck of the bottle before pouring. It's a particularly good idea for older wines.

Some wineries are phasing out these wraps, replacing them with plastic or other non-lead materials. However, older wines and some imports in the market still have lead foil caps. (One wine industry official quipped: "The only way that a lead foil cap on a wine bottle can hurt you is if you eat the darn thing.")

DRUG INTERACTIONS: Alcohol can change the effect of some medications, so always consult your pharmacist or physician about possible interactions. It exaggerates the effects of sleeping pills and other tranquilizers since it, too, is a sedative. Also, people who suffer drowsiness and impairment of performance because of antihistamines will find that alcohol increases this reaction. Further, it can aggravate gastrointestinal inflammation sometimes caused by aspirin.

Wine, women and health

There's that old gag about a liberated American woman trying to convince a Frenchman that too much was made of the differences between men and women; they were, she insisted, rather minor.

"Vive la différence!" the Frenchman exclaimed.

When it comes to drinking, there are *major* differences; women's bodies respond differently to alcohol intake. While studies show that women who drink moderately obtain the same cardiovascular protection and extended lifespan as men, the benefits appear to be evident after menopaus.

Women of all ages have a more pronounced reaction to alcohol. Since the average woman is smaller than the typical male and has less body fluid, her blood alcohol level will be raised more quickly. However, the differences go beyond that. Women have a higher percentage of fat in their body weight. Because alcohol isn't easily absorbed by fat, it tends to concentrate more in a woman's body fluids.

Further, studies show that a woman's bloodstream assimilates alcohol more quickly, and her body metabolizes it more slowly. Thus, the BAC level will elevate faster in a 125-pound woman than in a man of the same weight. She'll feel the effects of a drink sooner and will retain those effects longer.

A rather disturbing statistic emerged from one of Dr. Klatsky's surveys: Women who drink heavily are at a much greater risk for non-cardiovascular death than men. When compared with moderate drinkers, men who took six or more drinks a day had a forty percent greater risk, while in women, it was 160 percent! Many of these deaths were attributed to accidents and suicides.

According to studies quoted in the recent book *Women and Alcohol* by Moria Plant, Ph.D., women are more likely to abstain from drinking than men. They're also less likely to become problem drinkers. Dr. Plant noted that women were more inclined to be involved in temperance movements early in the twentieth century. On the other hand, many "women's tonics" of that era had high alcohol content. (Perhaps some of those temperance ladies were sipping Lydia Pinkham's Vegetable Compound behind closed doors.)

> *Statistics show that heart disease is the chief factor in thirty-eight percent of women's deaths, compared with four percent for breast cancer.*

BREAST CANCER: The medical jury is mixed where alcohol and breast cancer are concerned. A study of Spanish women published in the British journal *Cancer Causes and Controls* indicated that as little as one drink a day increased the risks of breast cancer by fifty percent. A Harvard study suggested that women who drink moderately decrease their chances of suffering heart problems but increase their likelihood of getting breast cancer at about the same rate. However, the American Cancer Society has said that occasional drinkers were no more likely to die of breast cancer than non-drinkers. A Department of Health and Human Services survey of 3,000 women with breast cancer and another 3,000 without it, found no relationship between moderate drinking and the disease. Similar conclusions were reached by the Framingham heart study in Massachusetts.

Even if there is a slightly increased risk, many medical experts think the trade-off is worth it. Statistics show that heart disease is the chief factor in thirty-eight percent of women's deaths, compared with four percent for breast cancer and ten percent for strokes.

PREGNANCY: Heavy drinking during pregnancy can cause damage to an unborn child, known as Fetal

Alcohol Syndrome. However, as with other heavy drinking scenarios, poor diet and smoking also may be factors. No studies have found a significant effect on fetuses for light drinkers. However, even pro-wine groups such as California's Wine Institute do not recommend drinking during pregnancy.

WRINKLING? At the risk of sounding like we're scraping the bottom of the health barrel, lab evidence now suggests that alcohol is involved in converting testosterone into estrogen in post-menopausal women. Loss of estrogen is a major cause of wrinkling in older women, so a higher level will slow this process, says Dr. Judith Gavaler, an epidemiologist at the University of Pittsburgh.

Testosterone in women? Yes, the male hormone exists in trace amounts.

To learn more about wine and health

A very useful booklet on alcohol and health issues is *Moderate Alcohol Consumption and Health* by the American Council on Science and Health, which we quoted frequently in the preceding chapters. While many groups supporting alcohol-and-health issues are industry connected, this one is not, so its findings can be accepted without prejudice. ACSH is a non-profit "consumer-education consortium concerned with issues related to food, chemicals, pharmaceuticals, lifestyle, the environment and human health." Its nucleus is a board of more than 250 physicians, scientists and others concerned with public health issues.

The organization publishes more than fifty health and lifestyle booklets including the one mentioned above. They were $5 per copy when we last checked; less for larger amounts. For a complete list, contact: American Council on Science and Health, 1955 Broadway, Second Floor, New York, NY 10023-5860; phone (212) 362-7044; FAX (212) 362-4919. (WEB SITE: www.acsh.org; E-MAIL: acsh@acsh.org)

Chapter nine

THE RIGHT MEASURE

Wine use without abuse

It would be intemperate and possibly even irresponsible to write a book celebrating the benefits of wine without reserving a few pages for some precautions. Anything taken to excess, probably including lovemaking, can be bad for your health. (That depends, among other things, on the marital status of your partner.)

Obviously, alcohol has a potential for intemperance, since it is an intoxicant—much more so than the scent of perfume in the hair of that other gentleman's wife. It is intoxicating because it's a depressant. Used in moderation, alcohol depresses anxiety, relieves tension, and eases inhibitions just enough to encourage camaraderie and perhaps a little daring in the *boudoir*.

Taken to excess, it inhibits judgment, common sense and coordination. It encourages people to dismiss their own sense of morality, and perhaps mortality. This depressant short-circuits warning messages, causing us to act without caution. Misguided high school kids who buy a six-pack of beer in order to get "high" are misusing the word. They are, in fact, getting low.

Dr. Arthur A. Klatsky, whose studies have demonstrated wine's health benefits, summed it up very effectively during an address at a meeting of the American Public Health Association:

The complex effects of alcohol drinking have always aroused strong feelings. Alcoholic beverages can be food and poison, boon and bane, blessing and curse, friend and demon, a healthy activity and a prelude to problems.

Abusers are losers

According to U.S. government statistics, eighteen million Americans are alcoholics. Many put themselves, their families, their jobs and the general public at risk. Irresponsible use of alcohol is involved in a third to a half of all traffic accidents, homicides, child and spousal abuses, suicides and drownings.

Fortunately, because of tough new DWI (driving while intoxicated) laws and better public education, alcohol-related accidents are declining. Drunk driving traffic fatalities have decreased more than twenty percent since 1977. They dropped four percent in just one year, between 1993 and 1994, according to the National Institute on Alcohol Abuse and Alcoholism.

Still, liquor is a factor in a third of all traffic deaths and nearly forty percent of all vehicle accidents. We are strong supporters of uncompromising drunk driving laws. They should be so intimidating that anyone who is over the limit will be terrified to touch the ignition key. As a police reporter in my younger days, I frequently witnessed the lethal results of drinking that got out of hand.

Wine is a minor player in the world of alcohol abuse. Less than two percent of those arrested for driving while intoxicated were drinking only wine, according to the Department of Justice. Wine is involved in only three percent of alcohol-related traffic accidents. Also, only three percent of alcoholics are wine drinkers; more than half drink beer and the rest choose hard liquor.

Thus, we have no qualms in defending peoples' right to drink wine—so long as they aren't driving. As for those who want to champion the cause of beer and hard liquor, let them write their own book.

All things in moderation

Since the science and health community loves to dwell on the word "moderation," we'll use it to suggest drinking guidelines. An ancient Arabic fable offered the same advice two thousand years ago:

When one first tastes the wine, and it begins to crawl in his limbs, the color blooms in his face, and he becomes as gay as a peacock. When the first signs of drunkenness appear, he plays, claps his hands and dances like an ape. When the wine grows stronger within him, he grows violent like a lion, challenging everyone around him. At last he wallows like a pig in the mire, desiring only to sleep, and his strength is gone.

To avoid the mire, it's best to keep your blood alcohol concentration (BAC) below .05. BAC is measured in milligrams of alcohol per 100 milliliters of blood. A milligram is 1/1000th of a gram and 100 milliliters is about 3.3 ounces. Blood alcohol content is abbreviated as mg%.

Generally, each drink elevates BAC by .02 mg% in a medium sized person (weighing about 160 pounds), so two and a half drinks within an hour would take you to .05. At this level, the moderate drinker begins to feel alcohol's euphoric effects. Intoxication sets in between .08 and .15 mg%. If levels exceed .30, the drinker goes into a stupor, headed for a coma and possible death as the alcohol suppresses vital bodily functions.

As we explained in Chapter Seven, a "drink" is about half an ounce of pure ethanol—the content of a five-ounce glass of wine, a 12-ounce beer, three ounces of sherry or port, or a 1.5-ounce jigger of eighty-proof liquor. Studies show that women physiologically are more affected by alcohol than men, even beyond their weight difference.

It takes one to two hours for your body to metabolize an ounce of alcohol, so anyone planning to drive should wait several hours after consuming two or three drinks. Pilots are more cautious, relying on their slogan: Twenty-four hours between bottle and throttle.

When drinking goes beyond the two-per-hour limit, your likelihood of having an accident increases dramatically—be it with an automobile, machinery or simply falling and hurting yourself. Statistics gathered by the American Council on Science and Health indicate that the risk of an accident increases by 100 percent at .05 BAC, by 600 to 800 percent at .10 and by 2,500 percent at .15.

The legal limit for motorists in most states has been .10 for years, although the federal government is pressuring them to reduce it to .08. Many have done so. Some DWI laws don't give you the option of trying to convince a judge or jury that you were not impaired, that you can "handle a few drinks." The laws simply state that it's illegal to operate a motor vehicle above a particular BAC level. Many states make it a crime for a motorist to refuse to take a blood alcohol test.

Since many motorists do imbibe—a drink after work or a couple of glasses of wine with a restaurant meal—we asked officials in the state with the largest number of cars for practical guidelines. These have been agreed upon by the California Highway Patrol and the state's Department of Motor Vehicles:

While it is recommended that a person who is driving not drink any alcohol, for those who choose to drink and drive, a suggested limit over a two-hour period is two drinks for a small person (90 to 129 pounds), three for a medium person (130 to 189 pounds) and four drinks for a large person (190 and beyond).

Food consumed with your drink slows alcohol's entry into the bloodstream. Wine has a social edge over other drinks, since surveys show that seventy-five percent of wine drinking in America happens at home. Beer and hard liquor drinkers are more likely to do their imbibing outside the home, and possibly operating a motor vehicle after having a few drinks.

Alcohol abuse—while certainly unwise—is not a major player in either natural or accidental deaths in America, accounting for about 7.6 percent, according to World Health Organization statistics.

Demon rum vs. the evil weed

Some temperance groups and politicians—and the federal government—tend to lump drinking and smoking together as common sins, to be penalized by restrictions and heavy taxation. Indeed, federal "control" of alcohol comes under the same branch that oversees tobacco and firearms. The idea that the same bureaucrats who dictate what can be on a wine label also determine what weapons of destruction are permitted in this country is laughable—although it isn't funny.

Alcohol and tobacco have almost nothing in common, except that both are federally controlled and taxed. Where alcohol has positive and negative characteristics, this can't be said of tobacco. If wine is currently the most studied element taken into the human body, then tobacco smoke must be a close second. And by every measure, by every study, smokers die earlier and suffer more health problems than non-smokers. It has been estimated that a third to a half of all cancer and coronary deaths can be attributed to smoking.

> *Nothing in this witch's breath of carbon monoxide, tar, nicotine, cyanide and formaldehyde has been found to be beneficial...*

Nothing in this witch's breath of carbon monoxide, tar, nicotine, cyanide and formaldehyde has been found to be beneficial to the body. Tobacco from any source in any amount has a negative impact on health. Fortunately, it's beginning to lose its death grip on American society. Lawsuits are dipping into the tobacco industry's profits and heavy taxation is taking more. One of the largest cigarette producers, R.J. Reynolds, has quit the business entirely, preferring to produce shredded wheat instead of shredding peoples' lungs.

With the passage of more stringent anti-smoking laws, it's tough to find a place to puff these days. However, we have no sympathy for you folks who stand shivering outside restaurants and offices, sucking smoke into your lungs. We're already helping pay your medical bills through increased insurance premiums; we don't want to inhale your tobacco fumes.

As smoking continues to come under the gun, we hope temperance groups, politicians and particularly the Bureau of Alcohol, Tobacco and Firearms will keep this thought in mind:

Moderate drinking is healthful while excessive drinking can be harmful. However, smoking in any amount is harmful.

A word on abstinence

We said at the beginning of this book that we aren't urging abstainers to start imbibing, despite evidence that moderate drinking offers health benefits for most people. If you have good reasons for not drinking, by all means continue your abstinence.

This question arises as we near the end of this section on wine and health: Is alcohol an essential ingredient to a good diet and longevity?

Of course not. As international surveys have demonstrated, many societies that drink very little alcohol outlive us. If you abstain from demon rum while following a good diet, keeping your weight down and staying in shape, you'll probably live just as long as we moderate drinkers, perhaps even longer.

Or, without that glass of Zinfandel to relax you in the evening, maybe it will just *seem* longer.

Part III:
WINE & YOUR DIET

Go thy way, eat thy bread with joy, and drink thy
wine with a merry heart.   **—ECCLESTIASTES 9:7**

Chapter ten

DINING WITH WINE

*Food with wine;
wine as food;
cooking with wine*

Wine's role as a faithful dining companion has been celebrated for centuries. Initially, this was because of sanitation, not culinary romance, since its resistance to bacteria made it the safest thing on the table.

Fortunately, poets soon took over and promoted it as something more significant than an antiseptic. Wine has four important functions at tableside. Its flavors can compliment the taste of the food, the sipping of it slows the pace of the meal, it helps you relax as you dine, and it gives you something to talk about.

Justin Meyer offers an interesting comment in *Plain Talk about Fine Wine*: "I think it's silly when people gulp down their food without ever commenting on it (and possibly without tasting it), and then swirl and sniff wine," turning it into a protracted ritual. To enhance the meal and aid digestion, both wine *and* food should be savored slowly.

Which goes with what?

I suppose we'd spoil all the fun if we said this business of matching wine with food is overdone. Of course it is, but what's the harm? Would you rather sit at the dinner table and discuss problems in the Mideast, or whether the Zinfandel has enough presumption to stand up to the pepper steak?

Furthermore, the *basic* rules of matching wine with food are logical. All the wine experts are really trying to tell us is that the ingredients of a meal should be balanced.

If the entrée is hearty and richly seasoned, the wine you serve should have a pronounced flavor as well. Your taste buds, flooded with spices and strong flavors of a *Chateaubriand*, won't be able to find the subtleties in a soft white wine. On the other hand, if you're having poached fish and want to taste its gentle flavor, don't drown it with a powerful young Cabernet.

From this logic has emerged an illogical generality: red wine with red meats and white wine with white. (And pink with pork?) However, a red wine such as a young Beaujolais can be quite delicate and soft; whites such as a fine Chardonnay often have very pronounced flavors. Thus, the real key to pairing wine with food is not to generalize, but to get to know your wines, an altogether pleasant pastime.

If you're dining out with friends and widely different entrées are ordered, you'll find several wines capable of keeping pace with diverse dishes. Soft young reds and *decent* rosés work with a range of foods, as does dry sparkling wine. Incidentally, we like to drink a very light red such as a Beaujolais slightly chilled to give it a bit more crispness.

One solution to mixed entrées is for diners to order individual wines by the glass, which many restaurants offer. However, many of them overcharge for these, so it's a costly way to pair wine with food. (A glass of wine shouldn't cost more than the wholesale price of the entire bottle, but many restaurants insist on following this evil practice.)

While you're matching restaurant food with wine, don't limit yourself to the entrée. If the place has a good—and reasonably priced—wine-by-the-glass selection, order different wines for appetizers, the main course and even dessert. The *sommelier* will be delighted to help, as he mentally fondles his growing gratuity.

A final word on dining out with wine: If you request a Zinfandel and the waitperson asks "red or white?" nod politely, get up and go to another restaurant.

Since writing and publishing isn't nearly as profitable as we'd hoped, I generally drink better quality jug varietals with dinner at home. (I don't drink generics; book sales aren't *that* slow.) Our everyday wine list features 1.5 liter Zinfandels, Cabernets, Merlots, Chardonnays and Sauvignons Blanc. It's difficult to play a precise wine-with-food match game at home. We tend to stay with whatever's open for several days until it's finished, so it's generally consumed with a variety of dishes. (Wine snobs may scoff at this practice, since that's the way most working class French and Italians drink. Keep in mind that, statistically, working class French and Italians outlive American wine snobs.)

Of course, I do have a supply of better wines laid away for special occasions, such as the vernal equinox, Bastille Day and the fact that the check from our book distributor arrived on time. However, most of these are reds and most of the reds are Zinfandels, so my cellar doesn't exactly burst with vinicultural variety. I have taught my taste buds that a light Zin is just fine with Betty's wonderful poached fish and stir-fried veggies.

The match game

Having said that it's not important to match wines with specific foods, we'll do just that. It's harmless fun, and the following pairings have stood the test of time. We have drawn them from a number of reliable sources, and even a couple of unreliable ones:

Lightly seasoned fish — Dry to medium Sauvignon Blanc, Chardonnay, Sémillon or Riesling.

Shellfish or seasoned fish — Medium Sauvignon Blanc, Chardonnay, Chenin Blanc, Gewürztraminer or Riesling.

Clear, light soup — Dry sherry or a very dry white wine.

Hearty soup or cream soup — Medium sherry, medium white or light red.

Lightly seasoned veal, young lamb, pork or poultry — A medium-bodied white or light red such as Beaujolais, young Zinfandel or a good rosé; a spicy Gewürztraminer also can work well here.

Turkey or ham with holiday meals — A variety of medium to full-bodied whites and light reds slightly chilled are fun accompaniments to Thanksgiving dinner, Yuletide feasts and Easter ham.

Spicier light meats, including ham — Medium-bodied Beaujolais, full-flavored Chardonnay, spicy Gewürztraminer, Zinfandel, Pinot Noir or Merlot.

Red meats, hearty stews, full-seasoned entrées and hamburgers — Full-flavored Cabernet Sauvignon, Zinfandel, Pinot Noir or Barbera.

Wild game or rabbit — Medium to full-flavored Zinfandel, Cabernet Sauvignon, Pinot Noir or Barbera.

White pasta — Medium whites and light reds.

Red pasta (including pizza) — Light to medium reds, especially young Zinfandel or Pinot Noir, plus Barbera and other wines with Italian roots.

Foods with which no wine works — We've found no satisfactory companions for anchovies, artichokes, asparagus, candied yams, chocolate, most egg dishes (because of egg's sulfur content), smoked herring, hot dogs, onions, pickles, pineapple, salads with oily or vinegary dressings, tomatoes (unless blended into a pasta sauce), plus curried dishes and spicy Indian, Mexican and Southeast Asian foods. For the highly-seasoned ethnic stuff, reach for the beer. If you're dining in an ethnic restaurant, order the beer from that country. Those folks know what works with their lively fare.

We end this study with two cardinal rules:

1: When in doubt, order a young Zinfandel.

2: *Never* drink white Zinfandel, unless you're stranded in the desert and the only other option is radiator water.

Wine as food

At many European tables, wine isn't just something to be served with food; it's *part* of the food. However, don't look for the four basic food groups, since wine alone offers limited nutritional value. It does contain a fair amount of B-complex vitamins, including riboflavin and lesser-known pyridoxine, nicotinic acid and pantothenic acid, all useful in nutrition. Wine also offers traces of the dozen or so minerals essential to health. Sweet reds are the richest in B vitamins and a glass of sweet or dry red will yield a fair supply of iron.

Wine rates second only to milk as the most complex biologic fluid, although we aren't claiming that it contains milk's major nutritional package. Taken alone, it falls far short of meeting minimum daily requirements. It is instead a useful *adjunct* to nutrition.

Since dry wines are low in sugars and contain no fat and little salt, they can help brighten a weight loss diet. Surveys have shown that wines don't contribute to weight gain even though a four-once glass has about 100 calories. A British study of overweight people revealed that, although wine sharpened their appetites and encouraged them to eat a bit more, it didn't result in weight gain or interfere with their weight loss. Wine increases a dieter's basal metabolism rate, which helps burn calories.

Many hospitals serve wine to patients, in order to enhance the uninteresting foodstuff that emerges from their cautious kitchens.

Cooking with wine

Wine as a recipe ingredient enhances the taste of food by imparting its own special flavors. Most of the great chefs of the world, and millions of lesser ones in millions of kitchens, use wine as an essential ingredient in their recipes.

Also, since alcohol evaporates at 175 degrees—well below most cooking temperatures—family chefs needn't worry about getting the kids juiced. Most of the wine's calories disappear as well, since they're primarily in the evaporating alcohol.

Many cooks suggest using wine to replace part of the water or other fluid that's called for in a recipe. Generally speaking, you need to use only a small amount of wine, since the evaporation of the alcohol and some of its water tends to concentrate its flavors.

Try using the same type of wine in your dish that you intend to serve with the meal. The resulting marriage of flavors will be wonderful! Never use a bad wine in cooking, since it will impart its inferior qualities to the dish. And *never* use a supermarket product labeled "cooking wine." Not only is it poor wine, it may be laced with MSG or salt, since laws require that alcoholic cooking wines be rendered undrinkable.

Here are a few cooking-with-wine suggestions, gleaned from assorted chefs, cookbooks and our own kitchen experiments:

☺ Use red wine as a base for the sauce in hearty beef stews.

☺ Also, use red wine as the sauce base when braising red meat in a crock pot or other slow-cooking process.

☺ Poach fish in a sauce made of equal parts of water and white wine, with herbs and spices of your choice.

☺ Add a bit of white wine to cream gravy.

☺ Use full flavored red wine in a marinade for red meats. It does wonderful things to a barbecue-bound steak and even hamburger!

☺ Use white wine in a fish or shellfish marinade.

☺ Add a bit of sherry, port or Madeira to baked custard.

☺ Sauté vegetables in dry sherry or white wine.

☺ Use dry wine as part of a salad dressing base.

☺ Use a bit of white wine in chicken or turkey stock, and a little red in beef stock.

☺ Experiment with a bit of dry sherry or white wine in soups. Sherry should be added just before the soup is served, before the fragrance escapes.

☺ To reduce the tartness of some dishes, use white wine when the recipe calls for white wine vinegar.

☺ Replace some of the water in court bouillon with white wine.

☺ Try red wine, perhaps blended with red wine vinegar, as a marinade for wild game to tame the flavor.

☺ When a recipe calls for herbs as seasoning, add a dash of white vermouth for accent.

Wine recipe sources

We were tempted to fill this slim volume with recipes, but then it wouldn't be quite so slim. Nor would we after testing them. We instead point you toward some excellent cookbooks that are health-conscious and/or focused on wine in cooking. Most of these can be ordered through your local book store—particularly one specializing in cookbooks. If not, try the address of the publisher we've listed after some of the titles.

Cooking With the Masters of Food and Wine by Kathleen DeVanna Fish, Bon Vivant Press, P.O. Box 1994, Monterey, CA 93942. This gorgeous coffee table book offers recipes from some of the world's leading chefs, including Julia Childs and Jeremiah Tower, plus those of wine experts and winery owners.

James Beard's Theory & Practice of Good Cooking; Alfred A. Knopf, New York. If you can find it on the shelves, you'll find a wonderful selection of recipes, many emphasizing the use of wine.

Jane Brody's Good Food Book; Bantam Books, New York. An encyclopedic guide based on cooking with healthy ingredients.

Choices for a Healthy Heart by Joseph C. Piscatella; Workman Publishing, New York. Another of the "heart-smart" cholesterol-lowering cookbooks.

Diet for a Happy Heart by Jeanne Jones; published by 101 Productions, distributed by Ortho Information Services, P.O. Box 5047, San Ramon, CA 94583. Wine is a frequent player in the health-focused recipes in this book.

The Diner's Guide to Wine by Howard Hillman; Hawthorn Press, New York. If you can find this out-of-print guide, it will lead you by the hand into the complex world of wine and food affinities.

Eater's Choice: Food Lover's Guide to Lower Cholesterol by Dr. Ron Goor and Nancy Goor; Houghton Mifflin Co., New York. A detailed study of health-oriented foods and recipes that use them.

Fields of Green by Annie Somerville; Bantam Books, New York. This vegetarian cookbook is based on recipes from the famous Greens Restaurant in San Francisco.

The French Paradox and Beyond by Lewis Perdue; Renaissance Publishing, 867 W. Napa St., Sonoma, CA 95476. Although this fact-cluttered book focuses on wine and health, it offers several recipes, many using wine as an ingredient.

Greens: A Country Garden Cookbook by Sheila Krans; Collins Publishers, San Francisco, Calif. Like *Fields of Green,* it focuses on vegetarian cooking.

Italian Country Cooking by Susanna Gelmatti; Ten Speed Press, P.O. Box 7123, Berkeley, CA 94707. This health-oriented book has dozens of recipes, from appetizers through main courses to desserts.

The Love Your Heart Mediterranean Cookbook by Carole Kruppa; Surrey Books, 230 E. Ohio St., Suite 120, Chicago, IL 60611. The focus is on the Mediterranean diet, and wine is rarely mentioned for some odd reason. However, the recipes are abrim with healthy, low cholesterol ingredients.

Savoring the Wine Country; Collins Publishers, San Francisco. This softcover book with color illustrations features recipes from such noted northern California wine country restaurants as Mustards, Domaine Chandon, Tres Vigna and Cafe Beaujolais.

The Sebastiani Family Cookbook by Sylvia Sebastiani; c/o Sebastiani Vineyards, 389 E. Fourth St., Sonoma, CA 95476. This fine cookbook by the matriarch of the Sebastiani family may still be available in the winery tasting room.

Wine in Everyday Cooking by Patricia Ballard, Wine Appreciation Guild (address above). This recipe book, with lots of useful marginal notes, was written by a professional cook and wine consultant.

Zinfandel Cookbook, Rhône Appétit and ***Companions at Table*** by Margaret Smith and Jan Nix; Toyon Hill Press, 118 Hillside Dr., Woodside, CA 94062-3521. Written by a noted cookbook author (Nix) and a Zinfandel enthusiast (Smith), *Zinfandel Cookbook* book focuses on "food to go with California's heritage wine." It has nearly 100 recipes and, not surprisingly, Zinfandel often is used as an ingredient as well as an accompaniment. *Rhône Appétit* features recipes that match Rhône style American varietal wines, while *Companions at Table* focuses on recipes and food to serve with American-grown Italian varietals.

Chapter eleven

LA MEDITERANÉE
The diet for life

The term "Mediterranean Diet" has become, in recent years, as much of a catch phrase as the French Paradox. Indeed, the two are closely linked, since most versions of the diet include wine with meals.

Just what is a Mediterranean diet? If you have a vision of a contented Italian family dipping slices of bread into olive oil, lacing their pasta with garlic and washing it all down with red wine, you'll be pretty close. Simplistic, but close.

Essentially, it's a back-to-basics approach to eating, a move away from processed techno-foods to the high carbohydrate, low protein subsistence fare of simpler societies. It could as well be called the Asian Diet, since traditional eating patterns of many Oriental countries are similar—although without wine in most instances.

A few decades ago, doctors and nutritionists wondered why so-called poverty level people in some countries appeared to have few health problems. As long as they weren't actually malnourished, the peasants of Italy, France, Greece, Turkey, Morocco and other Mediterranean countries outlived middle class people of the industrialized north. The same was true of rural people of China, Japan and other Asian nations. It obviously wasn't due to better health care, for medical services were minimal in many of these areas.

In recent years, studies have revealed the "secret" to their longevity: a simple high fiber, high carbohydrate diet of unrefined and unprocessed grains, fruits and vegetables. Meat is a rare treat among most peasants, since animals are poor food factories. It takes sixteen pounds of grain to produce a pound of beef, and subsistence farmers knew it made more sense just to eat the grain. By the same reasoning, an acre of land in China or Thailand is much more useful for producing rice than for animal pasturage. Only in the Western world can we afford to make room for those inefficient food producers we call farm animals.

Several years ago, an organization called Oldways Preservation & Exchange Trust of Cambridge, Massachusetts, working with the Harvard School of Public Health, started searching for the optimal diet. Using longevity records, they found that the people of 1960 Crete and southern Italy had one of the longest adult life spans on earth. Further, their rates of heart disease, cancer and other chronic ailments were among the world's lowest. Applying contemporary nutritional expertise to these old eating habits, they determined that these simple rural people had—by nature, necessity and accident—developed the ideal diet.

Oldways Preservation & Exchange Trust, incidentally, is a "non-profit educational organization that works internationally to preserve traditions and foster cultural exchanges in food, cooking and agriculture."

It's significant that the group looked to 1960's eating patterns to find the optimal diet. With the onset of modern food production and the spillover of fast food from America, the rural Greek and Italian nutrition level isn't as good as it was several decades ago.

From this lifestyle look at Crete and southern Italy has emerged the "Optimal Traditional Mediterranean Diet Pyramid." It was unveiled in early 1993 at the International Conference on Diets of the Mediterranean, held in Cambridge.

Traditional Healthy
Mediterranean Diet Pyramid

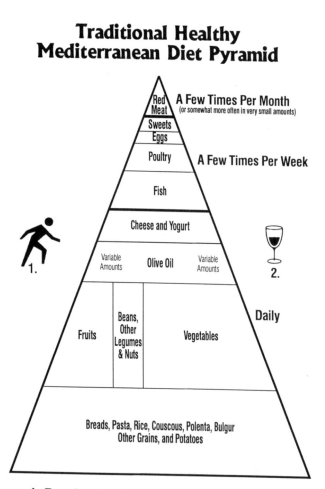

1. Regular physical activity is vital to maintaining good health and optimal weight.

2. Following Mediterranean tradition, wine can be enjoyed in moderation, primarily with meals (one to two glasses per day, for men and women respectively). It should be considered optional and avoided whenever consumption would put the individuals or others at risk.

SOURCE: International Conference on Diets of the Mediterranean; Oldways Preservation & Exchange Trust and Harvard School of Public Health.

The pyramid, duplicated here, shows that the foundation for their diet was ample daily rations of bread and grains, supported by plenty of fruits and vegetables. Topping out the daily portion of the pyramid—in smaller amounts—are beans and other legumes, nuts, dairy products (mostly cheese and yogurt), olive oil and olives. Also considered essential each day is exercise and a glass or two of wine. Working further up the pyramid, fish, poultry, eggs and sweets are recommended only a few times a week. Lean red meat is in the final tier, suggested *only a few times a month* as a special treat. There's no room at all for that marbled beef that's perfect for the barbecue!

(For a larger, more detailed version of the pyramid, contact: Oldways Preservation & Exchange Trust, 25 First St., Cambridge MA 02141.)

This pyramid turns the typical American diet into a complete somersault. Most families regard meat as the focal point of a meal, with vegetables as a side dish and salad as little more than a garnish. Olives are something we shake out of a can to dress up holiday fare. And most Americans don't serve wine with meals.

Many of us start our day with eggs and bacon, maybe grab a jelly doughnut at coffee break, and perhaps have a ham and cheese sandwich for lunch. We drive or take public transit to the job and back, getting very little exercise unless we're in a physical profession. Home from work, we ask what's for dinner, meaning what kind of meat are we having. Then we might grab a processed snack and a soft drink (twelve teaspoons of sugar) out of the refrigerator to tide us over until the steak or chicken is done.

Despite all the good news about nutrition and health, our diets actually have been deteriorating for generations. Surveys done several years ago for a *Newsweek* magazine article entitled "Fed Up!" revealed

---

Pyramid footnote: Olive oil, high in monounsaturated fat and rich in antioxidants, is the Mediterranean region's principal fat. In the typical Crete diet in 1960, it appears that total fat was safely as high as 40% of calories, with saturated fat at 8%, polyunsaturated fat at 3%, with the balance (29%) coming from monounsaturated (in the form of olive oil).

that half of us eat no fruit each day, and a quarter of us don't get our daily veggies. Fewer than one in nine get the daily recommended five servings of fruits and vegetables.

The quick food business is booming as never before. Several years ago, some fast food chains offered low-fat items along with their usual greasy hamburgers and french fries, but they sold so poorly that most have been withdrawn from the menu. The current mentality at McDonald's, Wendy's and other fast food outlets is that "bigger is better," as Whoppers and Quarter Pounders hit the takeout trays of America and the world.

Meanwhile, the processed food industry "processes" many of the nutrients out of natural foods, such as whole grains and other cancer-fighting fibers. They then add a few vitamins and minerals to assure us that their product is "healthy."

To give the industry credit, many food producers are listening to the growing ranks of diet conscious Americans. They're shifting from cholesterol-laden animal fats to more vegetable oils in their processing. They love to slap "no cholesterol" labels on their food products, even those that never had any in the first place. However, if you read the fine print, you may discover that many are heavy in saturated fat. Although plant-based foods contain no cholesterol, those high in saturated fat can contribute to triglyceride and cholesterol formation. Coconut, palm and other tropical oils often used to deep fry potato and tortilla chips are notoriously high in saturated fats. Seek out foods containing polyunsaturated or monounsaturated fats, which can lower "bad" cholesterol.

> *The current mentality at fast food outlets is that "bigger is better."*

Shelves are abrim with "no cholesterol" margarine to replace butter. However, margarine needs to be thickened for spreading, so many contain "partially hydrogenated" vegetable oils. Hydrogenation can change polyunsaturated fats to saturated, so you're right back where you started. Olive oil's monounsaturated fat, rarely found in butter substitutes, helps lower cholesterol, and it's rich in antioxidants that may help prevent cancer. Some food makers are returning fiber to processed foods (even using wood fiber) and many now tout the high-fiber content of their cereals. However, they may also add sugar to make the foods more palatable, adding to the problems of the millions of overweight Americans.

The Mediterranean Pyramid differs in several ways from the U.S. Department of Agriculture's Food Guide Pyramid, which you often see on food packages. It was adopted in 1992 to replace the outdated basic food group chart that you probably remember from your school days. The first two layers of the pyramids are similar, but the American version then inserts meats and dairy products at the next level, as daily staples for our diets. Furthermore, the American food pyramid has no level for olives and olive oil, and it doesn't recommend daily wine consumption.

Incidentally, the Oldways Mediterranean Diet recommendations aren't limited to Crete and southern Italy; these were chosen because they were closest to an optimal diet. Variations, with similar good health properties, are found in the rest of Italy and Greece, parts of the Balkans, Spain and Portugal, southern France, Turkey, Morocco, Tunisia, Lebanon and Syria.

"The geography of the diet is closely tied to traditional areas of olive cultivation in the Mediterranean region," according to an Oldways spokesperson.

The role of wine

Despite other studies showing longer lifespans among societies that drink little wine (Chapter Seven), creators of the Mediterranean Pyramid feel that it's a key to their diet:

Based on the results of extensive epidemiologic studies, it is unlikely than an optimal Mediterranean diet would be as protective against chronic diseases if moderate wine consumption were eliminated. The experience of traditional wine-drinking behavior in much of the southern European Mediterranean region, centered as it is around meals and typically within a family context, suggests that moderate consumption of alcohol need not lead to the myriad of alcohol-related problems witnessed in some other cultures.

Other studies seem to verify this latter point. According to World Health Organization statistics, for instance, the United States has seven times more alcoholics per capita than Italy, even though Italians drink nearly ten times more wine.

Why is wine a health key in the Mediterranean diet, and not in low wine consuming nations such as Japan? Perhaps the Japanese statistics are skewed upward by their excellent medical facilities and typical low-fat Asian diet. Would a Japanese farmer who washes down his tempura with a modest amount of saké outlive his urbanized teetotaling brother? Possibly; it would be interesting to find such statistics. We know of no such surveys, although other research suggests that the farmers of 1960s Crete did in fact outlive contemporary Japanese.

The elements of the diet

When you examine the composition of foods in the Mediterranean Diet, it's easy to see why those 1960s Greeks were among the longest lived people on earth. We'll take them from the bottom of the pyramid which, in a nutritional perspective, means from the top:

Breads, pastas and grains: These high-starch foods provide complex carbohydrates, the fuel that runs our bodies. They also furnish some of the essential fats we need, but not the kind that build fat cells and make us chubby. Unprocessed grains are an excellent source of fiber. The value of oatmeal in lowering cholesterol is well established. The high content of insoluble fiber in virtually all whole grains reduces cancer risks in the digestive tract by keeping things moving.

Fruits and vegetables: These are the great sources of vitamins and minerals, as well as high fiber, carbohydrates and natural sugars. All vitamins essential to health occur naturally in fruits and vegetables, except vitamin D, which our body produces and vitamin B-12, which comes from bacteria in our digestive tract. Since fruits and vegetables gather nourishment through their roots, they draw essential minerals from the soil.

Some veggies, particularly Brussels sprouts and cabbage, are good protein sources, and many are rich in antioxidants. You've probably heard about studies concerning broccoli's cancer-fighting capabilities, and it's long been established that carrots are high in the antioxidant called beta carotene. Other good sources are spinach, sweet potatoes, squash, cantaloupe and apricots.

Citrus fruits are good sources of vitamin C, also an antioxidant. It prevents scurvy, once the curse of mariners. Yes, it's true that British sailors were called Limeys because they were issued lime juice to prevent scurvy, as far back as 1795. There is ongoing medical speculation—never proven—that megadoses of vitamin C can fight the common cold.

Beans, other legumes and nuts: They're also excellent sources of carbohydrates and essential fats, and extremely good sources of protein. Vegetarians often rely on beans and nuts to ensure a good protein supply. However, food scientists tell us that we need much less protein than originally was believed. Some health officials caution against eating too many nuts because of their high fat content. On the other hand, many nuts are rich in vitamin E, an important antioxidant.

> *British sailors were called Limeys because they were issued lime juice to prevent scurvy, as far back as 1795.*

Cheese, yogurt and other dairy products: These are suggested daily, but only in small amounts. As pointed out earlier, there is some lab evidence that fermented dairy products such as cheese and yogurt bind to calcium and pass out of our system instead of hanging around to cause cholesterol problems. This has not been completely confirmed, although the French eat twice as much cheese as we do and still have their statistical paradox over us.

There is strong clinical evidence that the active bacteria in yogurt is a powerful antitoxin that helps win indigestion wars in the gastro-intestinal tract. Seven natural antibiotics have been isolated, and they're said to be more effective at fighting bacteria than terramycin. They're particularly strong against botulism, salmonella and staphylococcus. Yogurt is noted for its ability to calm an unsettled tummy. There is some evidence that it may be an anti-cancer agent, but this isn't conclusive. One study found that women who ate yogurt had fewer incidences of breast cancer than those who ate other dairy products.

You sweet-toothed folks must realize that those fruit-sweetened yogurts are very fattening.

Olive oil and olives: Could this be the magic ingredient of the Mediterranean diet? Olive oil is monounsaturated fat, which lowers LDL and helps maintain good HDL levels. In lab tests, a chemical in olive oil called *cycloarthanol* neutralized cholesterol before it could enter the bloodstream. One tablespoon nullified the cholesterol of two eggs.

Studies also suggest that olive oil may be an anti-coagulant that reduces the chances of blood clots. It's rich in antioxidants, mostly in the form of vitamin E. Some lab work indicates that its antioxidant qualities strengthen cell walls, making them less susceptible to oxidized free radicals that could trigger cancer. It has even been suggested that olive oil may retard aging by keeping cells alive and healthy longer. Other tests showed that two-thirds of a tablespoon of olive oil reduced blood pressure in men by four points.

Formulators of the Mediterranean Diet are so high on this stuff that they suggest using olive oil to replace all other oils in your diet, especially saturated and hydrogenated ones.

It would appear that olive oil even permits one to thrive on a relatively high-fat diet. Normally, dietitians say that no more than thirty percent of one's calories should come from fat. However, in the 1960 diet studies for the Mediterranean Pyramid, the folks in Crete were getting forty percent of their calories from fat, mostly from olive oil. Of course, people on very low fat diets also have extended longevity, particularly in Asian and some Latin American nations.

Garlic: Although it isn't mentioned in the pyramid, garlic is used as a common seasoning throughout the Mediterranean and parts of the Orient. Lab studies indicate that it reduces both blood pressure and cho-lesterol, stimulates the immune system and acts as an anti-coagulant. Some research has shown it to be an effective antioxidant, a possible factor in the Mediterranean longevity formula. However, lab tests reveal that you'd have to eat a pound of garlic a week to achieve an effective antioxidant level. It may keep you cancer-free, but you probably wouldn't have too many close friends.

Fish, poultry, eggs and sweets: These should be limited to a few times a week. The first three items contain cholesterol; sweets, while harmless to healthy people, will put on those pounds. They're also "empty calories," that take up space better utilized by more healthful foods.

Although dietitians recommend fish, poultry and "white" meat over beef, it's a myth that they're low in cholesterol. A 3.5-ounce serving of lean beef has eighty-five milligrams of cholesterol, but so does an equal portion of chicken breast, even with the skin removed. Turkey has only three milligrams less than chicken. Pork has ninety milligrams of cholesterol and veal has eighty-eight, both more than beef. Among seafoods, lobster comes in at seventy-two, trout seventy-three and smelt has eighty-nine milligrams. Most shellfish is exceptionally rich in cholesterol.

What makes red meat particularly bad for the old ticker is that it's high in saturated fats as well as cholesterol. So are veal, lamb and pork. Poultry is much lower in saturated fat, as is fish. However, if you leave the skin on chicken or turkey, it's nearly as saturated as steak. Fish is by far the best choice for avoiding cholesterol buildup.

> *Red meat contributes little more to our diets than protein, and we can get plenty of that from other sources.*

Some seafood is high in polyunsaturated fats called Omega-3, which can lower your cholesterol

Lean red meat: Sitting precariously at the tip of the pyramid, red meat contributes little more to our diets than protein, and we can get plenty of that from other sources. It has no fiber or complex carbohydrates and few vitamins. Our Mediterranean dietitians suggest that it be eaten only a few times a month. It should be consumed more frequently only if it's used in small amounts as a flavoring agent. Spaghetti 'n' meatballs, incidentally, is an American invention. In our travels in Italy, we never saw wads of hamburger in spaghetti sauce. In old Napoli where pizza was invented, you won't find it liberally sprinkled with pepperoni, sausage and certainly not Canadian bacon. A *real* Italian pizza is mostly a crunchy crust spread with a rich, spicy tomato sauce and cheese. Sorry about that, Pizza Hut.

Obviously, the Mediterranean Pyramid would be even more healthy if it were truncated; the world can live better without the red meat that occupies the pyramid's tip. Beef cattle consume hundreds of tons of grain that could be used to feed the world's needy.

Omnivores, not carnivores

The key to the Mediterranean diet is that foods from plant sources form the core, while those from animal sources are the fringe. Again, this is the reverse of the American diet. Taking a direct poke at the USDA suggestions, the Oldways Trust study concluded:

There is no reason to suspect that a Mediterranean diet might be deficient in protein or other essential nutrients, and every reason to conclude that such a diet would promote more of a reduction in chronic diseases than would the results of recommendations reflected in the USDA Food Guide Pyramid.

Other studies confirm that generous amounts of fruits and vegetables, augmented with limited dairy products, provide all the nutritional elements needed for optimum health—including calcium and protein.

Vegans, who eat no meat or dairy products, go a step further. They feel that milk or cheese aren't necessary to ensure an adequate calcium supply. After all, they reason, where do cows get their calcium to produce gallons of milk day after day? From plants, of course. They also point out that *homo sapiens* are the only mammals that continue drinking milk after they're weaned. There aren't too many calcium-deficient elephants strolling around. Some vegans insist that animal products are harmful in any amount.

We aren't convinced that nonfat milk is unhealthy. Only trace amounts of fat remains, and cow juice brims with good nutrients. We regard it as cheap insurance against calcium and protein deficiency, even though vegans and old elephants thrive without it.

Incidentally, when you see "low fat" and "two percent" on a milk carton, that doesn't mean that ninety-eight percent of the butterfat has been removed. As the son of a dairy farmer, I can assure you that most whole milk is about three and a half to four percent fat. Thus, two percent milk has less than half of the butterfat removed. Drink an extra glass, and you're right back where you started.

One of the great advantages of the Mediterranean diet is its diversity. It is not difficult to follow a regime that includes pasta with seafood sauce, spaghetti with all sorts of creative sauces, spicy stuffed grape leaves (*dolmas*), tasty Spanish rice, *polenta*, orange yogurt sauce, *bouillabaisse* or sautéed veal with peppers and garlic.

However, you can keep the smelly French cheese and *feta*.

Not only does a Mediterranean or Asian diet offer great diversity, it's less expensive than the meat-oriented American menu. If you like to cook, the variations are limitless. If you don't, it's a simple as boiling a pot of pasta or beans and building a fresh salad.

The American food industry won't like to hear this, but we don't need to engineer any more food products or develop new technologies to improve our diets. Nearly every attempt thus far has diminished the food's nutritional value, raised its price and—with its fancy disposable packaging—depleted our natural resources and added to our garbage heap.

If the food and agricultural industries are really concerned about health, they should concentrate more on increasing grain yields, then feeding it to the world's hungry, not to beef cattle.

Chapter twelve

Afterthoughts

A glossary of wine terms; other useful books

What did they mean by that? Virtually all disciplines, industries and areas of focused interest have their own languages.

Winetalk is particularly rich, curiously descriptive and—to an outsider—sometimes a little silly. To a winesmug, "nose" is what wine smells like, not the thing you smell it *with*. "Legs" are those rivulets running down the glass, and a winesmug can get very serious about their quality.

What follows is a winetalk lexicon. Commit it to memory and you'll know that a winesmug isn't insulting your wife when he proclaims: "Great nose and good body, but the legs are a little thin."

Acid — The tartaric and malic acids in a grape that give wine its crisp aftertaste.

Appellation — The term describes a legally defined grape-growing region, under the Approved Viticultural Area (AVA) system. For a label to bear an appellation designation, eighty-five percent of its grapes must come from that area, and the wine must have been "fermented, manufactured and finished" there. (Some states have more stringent percentage requirements than the AVA code.) Dry Creek, Carneros, Chalk Hill and Shenandoah Valley are typical California appellations. France's version—much older than ours—is *Appellation d'Origine Contrôlée* (AOC), which dictates the types of grapes that can be grown in each area. Typically, French wines are named for their appellation, while American premiums are named for the grape variety.

Apéritif (*a-PERI-teef* or *a-pear-a-TEEF*) — A drink taken before a meal as an appetizer; often a full-flavored but dry wine like vermouth or dry sherry.

Aroma — The smell of the grape from which the wine was made.

Balance — A catch-all term describing a wine in which nothing is out of balance: not too acidic, not too sweet, not too high in tannin.

Berry — To a vineyardist, grapes are berries; berry-like describes the flavor of the fruit in wine.

Big — No, it's not a large bottle. "Big" in winetalk refers to a wine with strong, complex flavor, full bodied and often high in alcohol. Tasters use the expression "big nose" to describe a wine with a strong aroma and/or bouquet.

Binning — Storing wine away, or "putting it down" for aging.

Blush — A term used to describe a pink wine made from red grapes, usually Grenache, Zinfandel, Cabernet Sauvignon or Pinot Noir.

Body — The fullness of a wine, which can refer to the viscosity or alcoholic content and/or the wine's complexity. A thin and watery wine lacks body.

Bordeaux (*bor-DOE*) — A large area of France that produces some of the world's finest red wines, usually blends of Cabernet Sauvignon, Merlot, Cabernet Franc, Malbec, Petit Verdot and Carmenere.

Botrytis cinerea (*bo-TREET-is sin-AIR-e-ah*) — A mold that wrinkles ripening grapes, causing a concentration of sugar and flavor that produces a rich, full-bodied wine. It's called "noble mold" by romantics and "noble rot" by cynical romantics.

Bottle sick — The condition of a wine immediately after bottling, when it has been filtered, shaken and otherwise abused. The condition passes after the bottle has rested a few weeks.

Bouquet — The often complex smell of wine that comes from fermentation and aging, as opposed to aroma, which is the smell of the grapes used in making the wine.

Breathing — The practice of letting a wine stand open for an hour or so before serving, supposedly to enhance its aroma and taste. It's done mostly with aged reds and experts disagree on its usefulness, but it's a harmless gesture to let your wine catch its breath.

Brilliant — Not a measure of the winemaker's cleverness, but the clarity of the wine. All good wines should be brilliant. So should a good winemaker, for that matter.

Brix — The measure of sugar content in grape juice, which will determine its alcoholic level upon fermentation; also the instrument used to measure it.

Brut (*brute*) — One of the driest of sparkling wines.

Bulk process — Cheap method of making sparkling wine by fermenting it in large sealed tanks to capture the carbon dioxide bubbles.

Cap — Layer of skins, pulp and other grape solids that floats to the top of a fermenting vat of crushed grapes. The winemaker "punches it down" or pumps the wine over itself to keep the cap broken up.

Cave (*kahv*) — French for cellar; it's "cava" in Spanish.

Chai — French word for a small building, usually above ground, for aging wine in small oak barrels. Some American wineries now use the term.

Champagne — A term describing sparkling wine in the United States. In most of the rest of the civilized world, it's applied only to effervescent wine produced in France's Champagne district. Some American winemakers honor this tradition and call their product sparkling wine.

Character — Term used to describe the good qualities of a wine. A poor wine, like a poor citizen, "lacks character."

Charmat (*SHAR-mahn*) — French term for bulk production of sparkling wine in sealed tanks, named for the Frenchman who developed it.

Château — Not necessarily a house, "château" is commonly used in France to describe a particular vineyard operation.

Claret — Usually referring to a Bordeaux in England, but used to describe just about any red wine in the rest of the world.

Coarse — A full-bodied wine, but with ragged edges and perhaps a harsh aftertaste; no finesse.

Cooperage — Wooden wine containers—barrels, vats and such.

Corky — A wine that has been invaded by a disintegrating cork, giving it a bad flavor.

Crush — It's often used as a noun in winetalk, referring to the harvest and subsequent crushing of wine grapes. "We had a good crush this year," a winegrower might say.

Cuvee (*Coo-VAY*) — A specific blend of wine, as in the "cuvee" used for a particular Champagne. Also refers to a vat or tank used for blending or fermenting wine.

Demijon — A large, squat wine bottle, sometimes covered with wicker.

Demi-sec — Sparkling wine with rather high residual sugar content; sweeter than sec.

Disgorging — Removing sediment that has settled in the neck of a bottle of sparkling wine; most of it is trapped in a small plastic *bidule*, placed there for that purpose.

Dosage (*Do-SAJ*) — The mix of sugar syrup, wine, brandy or other product added to sparkling wine.

Dry — Crisp and not sweet or sour. In winetalk, it has nothing to do with lack of wetness.

Enology — Winemaking science; one who makes wine is an enologist. Classic spelling is *oenology*.

Estate bottled — A wine in which all the grapes came from the vintner's "estate" or vineyards.

Fermentation — The reason for all this: the wine industry, winery touring, this book in your hand. It's the process of converting the sugar in grape juice into alcohol and carbon dioxide by the addition of yeast.

Fining — Clarifying wine to remove the solids, usually by adding an agent such as egg white that collects them.

Finish — The aftertaste of a wine, created primarily by the acid. A crisp, properly balanced wine will have a "long, lingering finish"; a thin, watery one won't.

Flowery — The aroma of a wine more akin to blossoms than to the grapes.

Fortified — A wine whose alcoholic content has been increased by the addition of brandy or other high-alcohol beverage.

Fruity — The flavor of a wine that comes from the grape.

Generic — A wine of no particular pedigree. In countries other than France, it is sometimes named for a wine-producing region, like Burgundy or Chablis.

Grapey — A wine that tastes too much like grape juice (think of Welch's). The grape taste should be subtle and is often described—particularly in reds—as berry-like.

Grassy — A subtle grass-like flavor, sometimes found in reds. It's sort of herbal without the herbs and not necessarily unpleasant.

Touring is a good way to add to your wine lore, then you can taste what you've been studying.

Green — A wine not ready to drink; too young; harsh and raw tasting.

Haut (*oh* or *auh*) — French for "high" or "upper," referring originally to wine-producing regions. Haut-Sauternes is a general term applied to a sweet white wine from upper Sauternes; the name has no bearing on quality. *Haut cuisine* might be literally translated as "upper class food." (Only the French would come up with a term like that.)

Hock — Generic term for white wine, usually used in England.

Horizontal tasting — No, it doesn't mean you've sampled too many wines. It's a comparative tasting of the same variety of wines from different vineyards or winemakers. Vertical tasting is sampling the same wine variety from different vintages.

Jerez (*hair-eth*) — A city and a wine-producing region of Spain; the birthplace of sherry.

Jeroboam — Oversized wine bottle holding the equivalent of six 750-milliliter bottles.

Late harvest — A wine made from grapes left on the vine until their sugar content is unusually high. This produces a full bodied high alcohol wine, and sometimes a very sweet one if the fermentation is interrupted to leave residual sugar.

Lees — Dead yeast cells and other sediment cast off by a wine as it ages.

Legs — This doesn't refer to Betty Grable's World War II pin-up pictures, but to rivulets that run down the side of a glass after you've swirled the wine. Firm rivulets indicate that the wine has good body, derived from its alcohol content and its complexity. A thin, watery wine will sheet down the side of the glass. Unlike Ms. Grable, it has poor legs.

Light — Referring to a low-alcohol wine or beer.

Magnum — A container twice the size of a normal wine bottle.

Maceration — A method of softening red wines after fermentation by letting them sit with their skins and seeds in hermetically sealed tanks for up to four weeks.

Malolactic fermentation — A secondary fermentation that occurs in wine, converting malic acid into milder lactic acid and carbon dioxide. This action, often occurring in reds, helps reduce their youthful harshness to create a softer, more complex wine.

Marsala — Italian fortified wine.

May wine — Sweet white wine, sometimes flavored with leaves or herbs; of German origin.

Meritage — A term used by a group of California wineries to designate red or white premium wines blended from classic Bordeaux grape varieties. Red Meritage is more common than white. A winery must join the Meritage Association to use the label, and it must meet strict blending criteria.

Méthode champenoise (*me-thoad sham-pen-WAH*) — The classic French method of making sparkling wine, in which it is produced and aged in the same bottle.

Methusalem — A king-sized wine container, holding the equivalent of eight ordinary bottles.

Micro-climate — Specific climatic conditions in a small area—a sheltered valley or exposed knoll—that make it ideally suited to a particular variety of grape.

Must — The liquid of crushed grapes, en route to becoming wine.

Nature — The driest of sparkling wines; in other words, one that is natural, with nothing added (although a small *dosage* usually is).

Noble grapes — The term, given somewhat arbitrarily, to the Cabernet Sauvignon of Bordeaux, Pinot Noir and Chardonnay of Burgundy and the Riesling of Germany.

Nose — The aroma and bouquet of a wine.

Oakey — A wine, usually red, with a strong flavor of the wood in which it was aged.

Off — Slang taster's term, meaning that a wine is "off base"; not "on."

Off-dry — A wonderfully silly winetaster's redundancy for slightly sweet.

Ordinaire (*or-dee-NAIR*) — French for ordinary; *vin ordinaire* is a jug wine.

Oxidized — A wine that has been exposed to air, and is starting to become vinegary (acetic).

Phylloxera (*fill-LOX-er-ah*) — Nasty little plant louse, 1/25th of an inch long, which destroys grapevines by attacking their roots. It raised havoc in America late in the nineteenth century and destroyed seventy-five percent of France's wine grapes. The scourge was stopped by grafting European varietals onto native American root stock, which is phylloxera-resistant.

Proof — Measurement of alcohol by volume, in which the proof number, for some odd reason, represents twice the alcohol content. Eighty-proof whisky is forty percent alcohol. The term isn't used in winemaking; wine is measured in "percentage of alcohol"—by volume, not by weight.

Proprietary wines — Special names given to a wine by the proprietor, usually reflecting place names or some pet fetish. They're almost always generic blends. "Riverside Farms White" or "Workhorse Red" are examples.

Pulp — A grape's fleshy part.

Punch down — The process of breaking up the "cap" or thick layer of solids that float to the top when a wine—particularly a red—is fermenting.

Racking — Clarifying a wine by drawing off the clear liquid from one cask or vat to another, leaving the lees and sediment that has settled to the bottom.

Residual sugar — The sugar that remains in a wine after fermentation to give it sweetness, usually measured by percentage. In sweeter table wines, fermentation is stopped by lowering the temperature to kill the yeast cells, thus leaving residual sugar. In dessert wines, brandy is added, which pickles the yeast and stops fermentation.

Riddling — Periodically turning and gently bumping sparkling wine bottles to work the sediments into the neck. It can be done by hand or with automatic riddling racks. This little wad of sediment, often gathered in a bidule that was inserted into the neck, is then removed by disgorging; see above.

Rotten egg — The harmless but yucky flavor of hydrogen sulfide sometimes found in a carelessly made wine.

Sack — Elizabethan term for sherry; thus the English brand name "Dry Sack."

Schloss — "Castle" in Germany, synonymous with France's "château" in describing a winery.

Sec — French for dry (not sweet), yet it describes a sweeter style of sparkling wine.

Secondary fermentation — Creating a sparkling wine by injecting sugar and yeast in a still wine and keeping it sealed (in the bottle or other closed container) so the carbon dioxide bubbles can't escape.

Sekt — German for sparkling wine.

Set — The appearance of berries after the grapevine has finished flowering.

Soft — A wine lacking harshness or rough edges.

Solera — The process of blending wines of different ages but the same type to achieve a consistency of style, commonly used to produce sherries. *Solera* refers not to the sun, but to *suelo*, Spanish for "floor," since the wines usually are blended from tiers of barrels, from top to bottom.

Sparkling burgundy — A sticky sweet drink made from nondenominational red wine. Once popular in America, it has fortunately fallen from grace.

Stemmy — An unpleasant green flavor to wine, as if stems were left in during fermentation.

Still wine — Any wine that isn't sparkling wine.

Sulfuring — Sterilizing wine casks or barrels to eliminate harmful bacteria, and dusting vines with sulfur to eliminate fungus.

Sur lees aging — The technique of letting white wines rest on their yeast lees (and sometimes other solids) for several months, resulting in the release of amino acids, esters and other compounds. This adds to the wine's complexity.

Tannic — Wine with the acidic flavor of tannin.

Tannin — Organic acids found in most plant matter. In wine, it comes primarily from the skins and seeds of grapes. Reds are higher in tannin because they're usually fermented with their skins. Tannin adds complexity and an acidic harshness to wine. Aging mellows these tannins while leaving the full, complex flavor. Tannic acid is used to treat leather, thus the word "tan."

Tartar — Those sparkly little crystals you may see on the underside of a cork are tartaric acid, which occurs naturally in wine and settles out during aging. If the wine is stored upside down, which it should be, the crystals settle onto the cork.

Tirage (*tee-RAJ*) — A French word with three definitions: *1.* The sugar-syrup yeast mixture added to still wine (*liqueur de tirage*) to begin secondary fermentation; *2.* Drawing off wine, usually from a barrel into a bottle; *3. En tirage* indicates bottles stacked for aging.

Topping — Topping off barrels of wine as it ages to replace that which is lost through seepage; otherwise oxygen would intrude and spoil it.

Varietal — A word you'll encounter thousands of times in this business. It simply means "variety," describing a wine made from a specific grape. Cabernet Sauvignon is a varietal; rosé is not. In most of Europe, wines are blended and named for the region in which they are produced. In America, wines are named for the primary grape therein. To be a "varietal," a wine must contain seventy-five percent of a particular variety of grape; some states require a higher percentage.

Vermouth — Yes, that stuff that adds zing to your martini is a wine. Vermouth originated in Germany and is flavored with assorted herbs and spices. The word comes from *wermut* or wormwood, whose flowers are used to add aroma. Both sweet and dry Vermouths are produced in America—mostly in California. In Europe, sweet Vermouth is usually made in Italy and dry Vermouth is associated with France.

Vertical tasting — Sampling several wines of the same variety from different vintages, usually from the same winery. Horizontal tasting is sampling the same variety of wines from different wineries.

Viniculture — The science of growing grapes for wine production.

Vintage — The year in which grapes of a particular wine were harvested. In America, a wine bottle can be "vintage dated" only if ninety-five percent of the grapes therein were harvested in that year. The harvest itself is sometimes called "the vintage" and the term "a good vintage" means it was a good year for a particular wine.

Viticulture — The science of grape-growing in general.

Vineyard designated wine — A varietal named for the particular vineyard where the grapes are grown; in America, ninety-five percent of the grapes must be from that patch.

Vitis labrusca — An American grape, found growing wild and used in early attempts at winemaking. It doesn't produce very good wine although its rootstock is resistant to deadly phylloxera (see above), so it became the base for many premium grapes.

Vitis vinifera — The source of most premium grapes. The vine grew wild in Asia Minor and likely was one of mankind's first cultivated crops.

OTHER USEFUL BOOKS

These publications will contribute greatly to your knowledge of wine appreciation, wine and food, and wine and health. Some are of recent vintage; others are out of print, although they may be found in winery gift shops or larger public libraries.

A Perfect Glass of Wine by Brian St. Pierre; Chronicle Books, San Francisco. This is an attractive, nicely photographed hardcover book about wines of the world and how to serve and enjoy them.

The Best of the Wine Country by Don and Betty Martin; Pine Cone Press, 631 N. Stephanie St., PMB 138, Henderson, NV 89014. A comprehensive guide to California's winelands, it lists nearly every tasting room from Mendocino County to southern California. The book also features nearby restaurants and lodgings.

The Common Sense Book of Wine by Leon S. Adams; Wine Appreciation Guild, 360 Swift Ave., South San Francisco, CA 94080. Longtime wine writer Adams calls this "the only book that de-mystifies wine without destroying its magic."

The Connoisseurs' Handbook of the Wines of California and the Pacific Northwest by Norman S. Roby and Charles E. Olken; Alfred A. Knopf, New York. The title says it; this thick paperback covers more than a thousand western American wineries.

Fireside Book of Wine by Alexis Bespaloff; Simon and Schuster, New York. A compendium of the many nice things people have said about wine, from Anton Chekhov to Art Buchwald.

Fruit of the Vine by Betty Dobson; Lexikos Publishing, San Francisco. This is a history of 200 years of California winemaking, with lots of historic photos and sketches. It's out of print but worth seeking.

Hugh Johnson's Pocket Encyclopedia of Wine; Fireside Books, 1230 Avenue of the Americas, New York, NY 10020. Issued annually, this slender and portable hardcover features wines and wineries of the world, wine and food and wine appreciation.

The New Encyclopedia of Wine by Alexis Bespaloff, Random Century Group Ltd., 20 Vauxhall Bridge Rd., London SW1V 2SA. An update of the classic by Frank Schoonmaker, the book answers every question you ever wanted to ask about wine, wine terms, winemakers and world wine regions.

Plain Talk about Fine Wine by Justin Meyer; Capra Press, Santa Barbara, Calif. This wonderfully earthy look at wine appreciation was written by the owner of Silver Oaks Cellars in the Napa Valley and northern Sonoma County.

The University Wine Course by Marian W. Baldy, PhD.; Wine Appreciation Guild (address above). For the serious wine student, this thick, scholarly paperback offers a complete home study course.

Vines, Grapes & Wines by Jancis Robinson; Reeds Consumer Books, Michelin House, 81 Fulham Rd., London SW3 6RB. This handsome hardcover book focuses on vines of the world and the wines made from them, with maps and attractive color sketches.

Wine: An Introduction by M.A. Amerine and V.L. Singleton; University of California Press, Berkeley, Calif. An early classic still in print, it's a scholarly, readable book on wine and wine appreciation.

Wine and Your Well-Being by Dr. Salvatore Pablo Lucia; Popular Library, New York. One of the first modern studies of wine and health, it's written with knowledge and good cheer. Published in 1971, it's worth looking for in used book stores or libraries.

Wine Country: California's Napa and Sonoma Valleys by John Dorper; Compass American Guides. This prettily illustrated softcover features wineries of America's two most famous wine regions.

Winemaking in California by Ruth Teiser and Catherine Harroun; McGraw-Hill Book Company, New York. This profusely illustrated coffee table book is scholarly, readable study of the state's wine history.

INDEX: Primary listings in *bold face italics*

Aerobic, 16
Alcohol, characteristics of, 14, 17, 18
Alcohol measures in drinks, 123
Alcoholics, 126, 130, 140, 141, 142, 150, 170
Alcohol-related traffic accidents, 60
Alzheimer's disease, 145
American Council on Science and Health, 9, 154
Anaerobic, 16
Angelica, 24, 54
Angina pectoris, 114, 132
Anti-bacterial action of wine, 143
Apéritif wines, *56*, 104, 177
Appellation, 31, 33, 82, 176
Appellation d'Origine Contrôlée, *31-33,* 35, 54, 177
Approved Viticultural Areas (AVAs), 33
Arteriosclerosis, 132, 134

Bacchus, 13, 21
Barbera, *42*, 159
Beaujolais (wine), 45
Beaujolais region, 32, 45
Biblical references to wine, 4, 11, 19, 20, 21
Black Muscat, 55
Blood alcohol, 146, 151
Bootlegging, 27
Bordeaux, 29, 32, 177
Bordeaux (wine), 29, 32, 43
Breast cancer, *147-148*, 172
Burgundy region, 30, 32
Burgundy (wine type), 30, 32, 50

Cabernet Franc, 98
Cabernet Sauvignon, 22, *43*, 98
California wine country, 60
Cancer, 133, *139*, 153, 165
Carignan, 44

Chablis, 42
Chablis region, 30, 32
Chablis (wine), 30, 38
Champagne (wine), 21, 47, *51-54*, 178
Champagne region, 32
Charbono, 50
Chardonnay, 22, *35*, 98
Charmat process, 52, 178
Chautauqua-Niagara wine area, 90
Chenin Blanc, *36*, 98
Chianti, 50
Cholesterol, 14, 18, 116, 118, *131-135*, 168, 172
Cirrhosis, 120, 122, 133, *141*
Claret, 50
Columbia Valley, 87
Cooking with wine, 160
Coronary artery disease, 111-118, 133, *136*, 153
Coronary thrombosis, 132

Davis aroma wheel, 97
Davis, University of California at, *26*, 41, 76, 98, 99, 110, 136
Dementia, 145
Demijon, 179
Dessert wines, 54
Diabetes, 142
Dining with wine, 106
Drug interactions, 146

Emerald Riesling, 41
Ethanol, 14-15
Ether, 18

Fermentation, 14, *15*, 30, 47, 50, 96, 140, 143, 179
Finger Lakes wine region, 91
Flora (wine), 41
Folle Blanche, 42
Food guide pyramid, 167
French Colombard, 37
"French Paradox," 7, 112, 117, *118*, 186

French wines, 22, *31-33*, 92, 110, 177
Fresno State Univ., 26, 110
Fumé Blanc, 37

Gamay Beaujolais, 45
Generic wine, 30, 33, *42, 50*
Geriatric health, 144
Gewürztraminer, *38*, 51, 98
Glycerol, 18
Gold Country wine area, 78
Gray Riesling, 39
Greece, 104, 164, 169
Greeks, 21, 113, 115, 170
Green Hungarian, 42
Grignolino, 46

Haraszthy, Agoston, 25, 49, 66
Headaches and wine, 142
Healthy living, keys to, 130
Heart protection tips, 134
Hippocrates, 114
House wines, 108
Hudson Valley wine region, 90
Hypertension, 135, *142*

Johannisberg Riesling, 39
J-curve, *121-122*, 125, 126
J-curve chart, 123

Klatsky, Dr. Arthur L., 8, 122, 127, 138, 150

Lactic acid, 16, 17, 18, 182
Lead in wine, 146
Long Island wine areas, 90
Longevity, 122, 126, 127, *129*, 154, 165, 172
Los Angeles, wine in, 24
Lucia, Dr. Salvatore P., 6

Madeira, 54
Malbec, 98
Malolactic fermentation, 17
Malvasia Bianca, 54
Marsala, 182
Martini, Louis, 27, 42

Mediterranean Diet, 113, *163-164*
Mendocino & Lake counties, 63
Meritage, 182
Merlot, *46*, 98
Mexico, 23, 24, 54, 66, 143
Méthode champenoise, 51, 182
Micro-climates, 182
Mission grape, 23, 54
Missions, California, 23-24
Mondavi, Robert, 37
Monterey County, 75
Muscat, 42
Muscat Frontignan, 54
Muscatel, 55
Myocardial infarction, 132

Napa Valley, 3, 36, 58, *68*
Nebbiolo, 50
New York wine areas, 88
"Noble grapes," 182
Northern Sonoma County, 36, *64*
Northern Willamette Valley, 82
Nouveau wine release, 45

Oldways Preservation & Exchange Trust, 9, 165
Olmo, Dr. Harold P., 41
Oporto, 56
Optimal Mediterranean Diet Pyramid, 165
Oregon wine areas, 81

Paracelsus, 18
Pedroncelli, John, 65
Petite Sirah, 46
Phylloxera, 26, 78, 182
Pink champagne, 53
Pinot Noir, *47*, 98
Pinot St. George, 50
Port, 56
Pregnancy and wine, 148
Prohibition, 20, *27*, 65, 78, 85
Proof (alcohol measure), 183
Proprietary wines, 30

Renaud, Dr. Serge, 113, 117, 136
Rhine (wine), 42
Romans, 20, 115
Rome, 21, 92, 104
Rosé, 28, 38, 48, *50*
Ruby Cabernet, 48

San Joaquin Valley, 26, 56
Sangiovese, 50
Santa Cruz County, 74
Sauterne, 42
Sauvignon Blanc, *40*, 98
Schloss, 183
Sebastiani family, 45, 66
Serra, Father Junipero, 23
Sémillon, 40
Sherry, *55*, 57
60 Minutes program, 7, 112, 119
Smoking & health, 130, 134, 152
Smoking & wine, 152
Solera, 184
Sonoma Valley, 36, 64, 66
South Bay (California wine area), 71
South Central Coast (California wine area), 76
Southern Santa Clara Valley (wine area), 73
Southwestern Oregon (wine areas), 84
Sparkling burgundy, 184
Sparkling wine, 17, 35, *51*
Stemmy, 184
Stemware, wine, 103
Storing wine, 104
Stress, 127, 136, *142*
Strokes, 133, *141*, 148
Sulfites, 14
Sylvaner, 42
Symphony (wine), 41

Tartaric acid, 14
Tasting wine, 95
Temecula Valley, 79
Tokay, 55
Treaty of Lisbon (wine appellations), 31
21st Amendment, 27

Umpqua Valley, 83
University of California at Davis, *26*, 41, 76, 98, 99, 110, 136

Vallejo, Lieutenant Mariano Guadalupe, 25, 66
Varietal wines, 35
Vignes, Jean Louis, 24
Vino Rosso, 50

Walla Walla Valley, 86
Washington wine areas, 85
Waterhouse, Dr. Andrew L., 8, 127, 137
Weight gain and wine, 143
White Riesling, 98
White Zinfandel, 38, 49, 51, 158, 159
Wine, taxes on, 13
Wine and dining, 106
Wine consumption per capita chart, 128
Wine glasses, 103
Wine in America, 22
Wine in history, 19
Wine Institute, 8, 9
Wine judging, 99
Wine label sample, 34
Wine myths, 109
Wine pricing, 106
Wine recipe sources, 161
Wine storage, 104
Wine tasting, 95
Wine scorecard, 100
Wine with food, 157
Winery touring, 59-60
Wine's components, 14
Wine's nutritional characteristics, 159
Women and wine, 28, 123, 141, 142, *146*
Women's Christian Temperance Union, 88
Wrinkling and wine, 148

Yakima Valley, 87
Yeast cells, 16, 52

Zinfandel, 30, *48*, 56, 98

MORE GREAT TRAVEL BOOKS!